21St CENTURY ZERUBBABELS

Building the Foundation Of the Temple

The Lord rejoices to see the plumb line in Zerubbabel's hand.

DON ATKIN

Cover Design by Denise Douglas
www.jdimagery.com

The Amplified Bible Classic Edition (AMPC) was the first Bible project of The Lockman Foundation. It attempts to take both word meaning and context into account to accurately translate the original text from one language into another. The AMPC does this through the use of explanatory alternate readings and amplifications to assist the reader in understanding what Scripture really says. Multiple English word equivalents to each key Hebrew and Greek word clarify and amplify meanings that may otherwise have been concealed by the traditional translation method. The first edition was published in 1965.

The AMPC is based on the American Standard Version of 1901, Rudolph Kittel's Biblia Hebraica, the Greek text of Westcott and Hort, and the 23rd edition of the Nestle Greek New Testament as well as the best Hebrew and Greek lexicons available at the time. Cognate languages, the Dead Sea Scrolls, and other Greek works were also consulted. The Septuagint and other versions were compared for interpretation of textual differences. In completing the AMPC, translators made a determined effort to keep, as far as possible, the familiar wording of the earlier versions, and especially the feeling of the ancient Book.

The AMPC present on Bible Gateway matches the 1987 printing.

"I have appointed you
this day over the nations
and over the kingdoms . . .
to build and to plant."

Jeremiah 1:10

You are God's field,
God's building

1 Corinthians 3:9

From every tribe and tongue
and people and nation

Revelation 5:9

COMMENTS AND COMMENDATIONS FROM TWELVE APOSTLES

Preparing this critical diagnosis of a church on life support, and the radical prescription for corporate health and integrity, I asked several apostles to read this book before publication. I have been greatly encouraged by their responses:

"I certainly appreciate Don's directness in his new book *"21st Century Zerubbabels."* Many who serve the church are aware of fallacies which exist in contemporary church. Don points those out, but as I have seen him do in the past, he does so with love. Don knows well that he is speaking of the bride of Christ. Therefore, he very carefully offers biblical solutions to those issues. So as the church moves forward captured by the power of the Holy Spirit, his book puts hope in my heart that the church of Jesus Christ will even in my lifetime rise up to honor Christ, its head. Then we can pass to the next generation an amazing glorious church that reveals to this world the heart of our loving Father. Please make this a slow soaking read, if not you might miss some of the treasure contained within." – **Steve Bishop**, Chester, South Carolina

***

"'Behold, I am going to send My messenger, and he will clear the way before Me. And the Lord, whom you seek, will suddenly come to His temple; and the messenger of the covenant, in whom you delight, behold, He is coming,' says the LORD of hosts.

"As the above verse was said of John in Scripture, with the compilation of the truth in this book, the same applies to Don Atkin, who challenges the church to a most necessary rethink of its apostolic condition and apostolic priority, as illustrated in the following two quotes of many accurate ones found within:

- Only when people have first place in our ministerial agenda will we be rightly ready to represent the King and His glorious kingdom. As His love "leaks" through our brokenness, others will know that we care.

- We have been content to live beneath the apostolic level. We have not felt this kind of requirement of character to be incumbent for us, and therefore we have been satisfied to be 'nice guys,' or our standard is a standard of 'Christian respectability,' and of being pleasant and polite. But I want to ask you a question: Is our gospel going forth in the power of the Spirit, and in full conviction?

"As you read and are moved in your heart, may His highway be prepared through your being, as we're placed collectively to reveal his Glory! Thank you Don!" **Owen Boyce**, (The Republic of) Trinidad and Tobago, West Indies

***

"I don't know about anyone else, but *"21st Century Zerubbabels"* is, for me, the vision or mirror of apostle Don Atkin's heart. BUT that's not what I saw or what caught my attention; the book itself was not what stirred me. The *tone* of the book and the HEART of Don is what really got me. I felt something reading this book. I felt the heart of Don. It was as if a father was writing his children with such a desire and passion to 'get it.' Much of what he wrote was like humble confessions and, though penned, written not with ink by the Spirit in Don. It was the humility of the soul, and very life of Don imparting not only the Gospel, but, as Paul said, 'So being affectionately desirous of you, we were willing to have imparted unto you, not the gospel of God only, but also our own souls, because ye were dear unto us.' (1 Thess. 2:8). All I could think of was Malachi 4:6, of the Lord turning the hearts of the father to the children. I felt this book. I felt Don's heart. I felt the heart of God the Father. And I cried reading this book because, 'I got it!' And I hope you get it too." – **Ricardo Butler,** Orlando, Florida

***

"A very special book." – **Ron Cottle**, Columbus, Georgia

***

"Wow Don. Your books always challenge me to want to be more like Christ. I love this book. I want to live my life accordingly. I am going to recommend this to everyone I know. The truth you have shared here is desperately needed if we are going to see a glimpse of what the Lord has in mind for His church in our lifetime. Thank you for a book that gives hope, much hope, that Jesus is indeed building the whole church, not just the part I'm involved in!" – **Richard Hamm**, Kingsport, Tennessee

***

Personality cults abound in the 21st Century Church. In *21st Century Zerubbabels,* Don Atkin cuts to the core issue of Church reformation; namely, the emergence of the true fivefold ministry, especially apostles, who possess the plumb line of God. I Chapter 4 of Zechariah, drawing on the prophetic testimony about Zerubbabel, Don lays out a framework for evaluating the true leadership from the false while issuing a challenge to current church leadership

The true apostolic refuses to be celebrated while Christ is being ignored, for Christ is the only message. This was the crux of the matter in 1 Corinthians 1 when Paul grieved over the divisions based on personalities in the early church. The true mark of the apostolic in this hour is its ability to lead the way while staying out of the way. Unless men and women believe that Christ is the one building His church, they will continue to usurp Christ's authority, drawing people after themselves. They will gum up the works and hinder the progress of the Kingdom. God is asserting His Lordship among His people. Right now this message is focused on leaders, that they might not be found building their own kingdoms or receiving praise that belongs to Christ alone.

Read this book on your knees. Pray that God will cause you to walk worthy of your calling – **Brian Harrison**, Meridian, Idaho

***

"Well done, Don. You have captured and expressed the heart of our Lord Jesus Christ. You truly are an 'elephant slayer.' This truth is necessary for the advancing of His kingdom. Egos, elephants and expectations that are self or other-centric have to be exposed and brought down through the power of His nature, which is love. I believe this book is a stone in the sling of a Davidic company to bring down a giant elephant that is in the midst of His people, crushing many of them.

"Jesus did only what he saw Abba doing (Jn 5:19). He spoke only what He heard Abba saying, for His words are spirit and life (Jn 6:63). In light of this truth, we hear Jesus' prayer in John 17:21, *'that all of them may be one...'* He then continues to define and qualify that 'oneness' so it won't be left to our imagination or will. This is our Chief Apostle.

"Genuine apostolic order advances the kingdom of God by establishing His will on earth as it is in heaven (Mt 6:10). It was God who created the unity of the spirit and commanded us to keep it (Eph 4:3). This is necessary in restoring the apostolicity of His church." - **Ron King**, Toledo, Ohio

***

"This message is greatly needed. I deeply appreciated the theme and the emphasis on one church, humility, servant leadership, collaboration and team work. I am in heartfelt agreement with the message and spirit in which the message is presented." – **George Kouri**, Jacksonville, Florida

***

"The notion that we are supposed to be about 'building' the Lord's House is not supposed to be a faith-fantasy reserved for the quiet confines of prayer meetings — but an absolute mandate given to us by the Lord Himself. His purpose in giving us gift ministry in Ephesians 4, to both lead and orchestrate such 'building' is just one of the implications that He fully expects it to be done. Don has done an awesome job in identifying the spirit that is needed to make it happen. If you long for such a time—where we can see such unity of mind for purposeful building rather than the selective camping and ostracizing that is regular occurrence within the Body of Christ—read, pray, and then act. I appreciate the challenge Don gives us to not surrender our progression in the faith to the whims of the soul. True leaders, and dare I say true apostles, will find this book refreshing." – **Jimmy Mas**, Tamarac, Florida

***

"A big endorsement to all you are saying! No reservations or qualifications. You're on the money Don! Keep firing!"
– **David Orton**, near Melbourne, Australia

***

"This is perhaps the biggest challenge for the church of the 21st century. How long will we allow history to repeat itself?"
– **Kobus Swart**, Cape Town, South Africa

***

"Don Atkin has delivered a timely apostolic entreaty for the church to rise beyond our ecclesiastical traditions which keep us divided. He calls for 'eclectic' Zerubbabels who, by the Spirit of Wisdom, know how to craft and engage the 'relational infrastructures' that will break down the walls that keep us apart. The church of Jesus Christ stands at a very critical, pivotal juncture. Will we continue to only perpetuate the gospel of salvation from a self-preservation stance? Or will we choose to embrace the gospel of the Kingdom—His purpose, His passion, His heartbeat?

"Don has powerfully dismantled the 'us and them' mentality, the idols of dogma, our traditional mentalities and customs. May we heed the upward call, that history not repeat itself, that principalities and powers not reign supreme in our localities any longer. May the Love of God prevail. May relational dynamics be realized and prioritized. May we fully embrace the mind of Christ, the unity of the faith. And may we be lifted above our human tendencies of trying to control each other, trying to change each other!

"Thank you, Don, for speaking directly to our hearts, for dealing with these issues, and for challenging us. If embraced and received with understanding, *"21st Century Zerubbabels"* will bring about city-wide and global transformation of the church as we know it, and will lead to 'The One Corporate Man' being an actual reality in the earth." – **Collin van Rooyen**, Durban North, South Africa

FROM OTHER ELDERS & EQUIPPERS

"Reading this was so encouraging to me because it is evidence that the Lord is raising up voices to disrupt our present paradigms, and point us back to Himself and to the Scriptures, to realign us to His ways to achieve His plans.

"I feel this book (and many other of your writings) is not something to read through and check off the list that you've read it, and go on. No, it needs to be read through a couple of times, underlining and noting what will be disruptive to the status quo. Then, get with others to look into the Word, seeking the Lord TOGETHER, listening to the Spirit. And then taking real steps to align with what is revealed.

"Change is needed, and it starts with a courageous few taking the first steps (and some are already on the way), then staying the course. The time is now!" – **Phil Carlson**, Chicago, Illinois

***

"Perhaps the most valuable component of *21st Century Zerubbabels* is Don's assessment of the current state of the church, and of what inhibits her from maturing into the beautiful bride she's destined to become. It is a perspective informed by decades of pouring his life into the mission, and is filtered through a humble heart that yearns to be part of a body that is truly one. Anyone who knows Don knows that his life bears the fruit of this message. Regardless of whether more discussion about 'apostolic ministry' is something that pique's your interest or turns you off, you might want to start with the book's Appendix, which is an excerpt from the Art Katz' book, 'Apostolic Foundations.' It sets the standard for what it means to be an authentic "apostle" and is likely to challenge the legitimacy of what you may have witnessed or experienced in the past. Ultimately, there is much within the rest of the book to challenge the status quo, but moreover, it is a heart cry to rise above our shortcomings and to step into the corporate identity that has been ordained for us." **Bryan Corbin,** Chillicothe, Ohio

***

"This past season, God has led us to study Zerubbabel, and the rebuilding of the temple, as a guide for what He wants to do in us. The sentence that has stayed with me and defines the cry in my heart is, 'We have planted but not built.'

"When you came to Mallorca over 10 years ago you shifted our paradigms. We were immersed in the gospel of salvation but no one ever showed us the gospel of the Kingdom. You were sent and we were built. I remember the afternoon I asked you if you could pray for me to receive the revelation of the Kingdom and you said, 'If you want it, it is yours.' That moment has defined my adult life." – **Damaris Amador Moll**, North Saanich, British Columbia

***

"In your book, *'21st Century Zerubbabels,'* the thing that really stands out for me is the valley of dry bones shown to Ezekiel in which he is asked to prophesy over this seemingly dry and dusty graveyard and as he did God raised up a great army of His people. I don't know how God will orchestrate such a powerful move but I know one thing that the unity of the Spirit among the brethren and the "Prophetic Proclamation" spoken by these 21st century Zerubbabels will in fact play a gigantic part in the creation of the true temple of last days living stones! Your book holds much insight on the restoration of those things which must be addressed in order for the church of the last days to come together in the unity of the Spirit! May God bless you and increase your revelation! Thank you for sharing," – **Tim Laughlin**, Ft. Worth, Texas

***

"It is not too often that you have opportunity to read a book from a seasoned veteran in church planting and nurturing that can look beyond the things that divide the church and find the scriptural basis for that which unites the church. Don Atkin is such a man. Having known him for many years I know that his reputation as a man of God is excellent. And his words come with wisdom from the Lord.

"Read this book with an expectation to learn things that you do not know yet or that you will see with a new perspective. Don's heart of the apostolic father runs throughout and his particular insights spring from many years of experience of sometimes doing it the wrong way and years of seeing God doing it afresh and anew, both in American and foreign cultures. Whether young or more seasoned in ministry you will be both challenged and encouraged."
– **Kent Phillips**, Franklin, Tennessee

***

If we are willing to lay down our historical and all-too-habitual prejudice and be willing to fully comprehend the role and functions of the apostle, we would be amazed at how the Western church has been able to sustain itself for over seventeen centuries without a fully legitimized form."

From "The Permanent Revolution" by
Alan Hirsch and Tim Catchim

CONTENTS

Comments and Commendations   5

Foreword   19

Theses   21

Preface   25

Introduction   27

Chapter 1   PROPHECY & PURPOSE UNFULFILLED   33

Chapter 2   THE ELEPHANT IN THE ROOM   39

Chapter 3   DRY BONES   45

Chapter 4   LIKE A MIGHTY WIND   51

Chapter 5   EQUIPPERS & KINGDOM ACTIVITY   57

Chapter 6   A FRUIT-BEARING NATION   61

Chapter 7   WAYS OF RELIGIOUS MEN   69

Chapter 8   THE SPIRIT OF ZERUBBABEL   77

Chapter 9   THE TEMPLE & THE TOP STONE   83

Chapter 10   DIVINE TREASURES IN EARTHEN VESSELS   91

Chapter 11   GIFT MIX & SPIRITUAL DNA   99

Chapter 12   ABOUT PROPHETS & TEACHERS   105

Chapter 13   ECCLECTIC WORKERS NEEDED   115

Chapter 14   HOLISTIC APOSTOLICITY   121

Chapter 15   KINGDOM ECONOMICS 101   127

Chapter 16   KICK THE CAN OR CHANGE COURSE   133

Appendix 1   LEADER-SHIFT by David Orton   137

Appendix 2   APOSTOLIC CHARACTER by Art Katz   139

"Jesus proclaimed the kingdom of God . . . and what came was the church."

French biblical scholar
Alfred Loisy

WHAT IS INSTITUTIONALISM AND HOW DOES IT AFFECT THE CHURCH?

S. Michael Craven

Prior to Constantine, the church, although organized, was less institutional and more communal or organic. In other words, the outside world didn't think of "the church" as that building on the corner. Instead they thought of a community of people who were distinct in both their conduct and character, the overarching characteristics being their love for others, compassion toward the needy, and joy-filled lives. The early Christians lived with hope and shared their hopeful vision of life and a world made better by the redemptive work of Jesus Christ. These Christians saw the world through Jesus' tearful eyes, seeing that things were not as they should be. This vision would shape their mission and purpose as they worked to bring the redemptive power of Christ and His kingdom to bear on every aspect of life and society. These Christians, through reliance upon God, would change the world!

Over the centuries, however, this would change. First, the marriage between church and state would lead to the concentration of social, cultural, and political power-power that corrupts. It was this condition that, in large part, would spark the Protestant Reformation. Then came the Enlightenment, with its emphasis on human reason and ingenuity. Over the years, the influence of the Enlightenment would elevate man's role in human affairs and diminish the role of the Holy Spirit and the reality of Christ's kingdom. Increasingly within the church, men would come to rely more on management techniques and human strategies (i.e., the tools of modernity) to fulfill the church's mission on earth.

Today, the managerial and therapeutic revolutions of the twentieth century have come to dominate. As a result, the church is less communal, less organic, and more institutional. We have become reliant on marketing techniques and programs and tend to treat the church as a mere organization to be maintained and managed as opposed to a supernatural life to be lived together under the rule and reign of God. This cultural accommodation is perhaps our greatest (and least recognized) and has rendered the church and its mission less relevant and devoid of any real power to influence the world.

The solution, in my opinion, is to repent of our reliance upon the tools of modernity and seek first the kingdom. Practically speaking, this means we must recover the reality of God's kingdom come to earth-those paradoxical virtues that teach that real power comes from God as expressed in the abandonment of worldly power, eagerly offering forgiveness, seeking others' welfare rather than our own, and loving others without conditions. The reality of our salvation into God's kingdom should lead us to trust not in our own understanding but live instead as children dependent upon God-by following in the radical way of Jesus.

We must resist the temptation to do for God and learn once again to abide in Christ, allowing him to transform us into holy children of the Living God who have received new lives that display His power and character. This is the radical way of Jesus and there is simply no other way in which the church can be truly faithful to its mission.[1]

.

---

[1] S. Michael Craven, Christian Post Guest Columnist, February 2013

40
THESES

40 THESES

1. Jesus Christ is the only begotten Son of God, the firstborn among many brothers.
2. Jesus Christ is Redeemer of the fallen world.
3. He purchased for God men from every tribe and tongue and people and nation.
4. They are, individually and corporately, a new creation, born of and led by God's Spirit.
5. The new creation embodies the Spirit and life of Christ.
6. Jesus has made them to be a kingdom and priests to our God.
7. They will reign upon the earth.
8. The Gospel of the kingdom on earth as it is in heaven is to be proclaimed in the world.
9. The church is to disciple the nations.
10. The church is to be the visible expression of Christ and the model of His kingdom in every locality.
11. God has one house with many places.
12. There is a specific place for each believer in God's house.
13. God places us in His house as He wills
14. God graces and gifts every believer for a specific work.
15. Each believer is to walk in the works prepared for him.
16. God has given gifts of apostles, prophets, evangelists, shepherds and teachers.
17. These gifts are to equip the church members for works of service.
18. These gifts, working together, are to bring the individual members to maturity.
19. The many members are to be one fully constituted and functional body in each locality.
20. They are to be fitted and held together by what each one supplies.

21. They are to be subject to one another in the fear of God.
22. Together, true believers constitute a royal priesthood.
23. They are a holy nation.
24. They are God's people.
25. God spoke long ago to the fathers in the prophets.
26. Today, God has spoken to us in His Son.
27. The just shall live by faith.
28. Faith comes by hearing Him.
29. Faith works by love.
30. Without faith, it is impossible to please God.
31. Jesus Christ is the Apostle and High Priest of our confession.
32. He is the prototype for all apostles
33. God has appointed in the church, first apostles, second prophets, third teachers.
34. The church is to be credibly constituted and ordered as one expression within each locality.
35. Until apostolic order is honored, the church will not be credibly constituted.
36. Until the church is credibly constituted and ordered,
    a. The purpose of God will continue to be aborted
    b. The kingdom of God will not be realized on earth as it is in heaven
    c. The gates of Hades will not be threatened
37. The church is both the embodiment and the bride of Christ in every geopolitical sphere.
38. The fully legitimized form of church manifests the oneness and love that is known by the Father, His Son, and His Spirit.
39. The fully legitimized form of church is the fruit of holistic apostolicity.
40. The gates of Hades will not overpower the church that Jesus is building.

PREFACE

By Watchman Nee

Here is a small portion of Watchman Nee's Preface to "The Church and the Work." It is exactly the preface needed for the book that you are just beginning to read.

The book is not intended for anyone and everyone. It is for those who bear responsibility in the Lord's service. But, more than this, it is for such as honestly and truly mean business with God, for those whose hearts are open and have no padlocked mind or prejudices. The book may test one's sincerity and honesty to no small degree; but genuine hunger and desire to know the Lord's full thought will sustain the perusal to the end. I fully realize the many imperfections of this book (this is not a gesture, but a confession); but despite them all, I believe the Lord has shown something which is of importance to the whole Body of Christ. The whole matter will grow upon the reader and become clearer with relaxed contemplation after the first reading. The door must not be closed with a snap of "Impossible!" or, "Ideal, but not practical!" By prayerful openness of heart, without argument or discussion, the Spirit of Truth should be given a chance, and then what is of Him will cause all our natural reactions to die away, and we shall know the Truth and the Truth shall make us free![1]

---

[1] WatchmanNee.org

It isn't that they can't see the solution.

It's that they can't see the problem.

G. K. Chesterton

INTRODUCTION

Among Nee's many contributions is a three-volume series entitled "The Church and the Work," a comprehensive clarification between the local church and the apostolic company. Over the years since Calvary and that following Pentecost, that delineation has disappeared. The essential and unique function of apostles has been so completely marginalized that their grace to bring God's people together has been abandoned, and most have retreated within their own organizations with the likeminded.

If there is to be a permanent revolution, the dramatic transformation which many believe is needed; there will first need to be a rediscovery of the essence, integrity, and interactions of these two vital parts of God's intention—the *church* and the *work*.

For us to rightly embrace the purpose of this writing we must first come to grips with the core issues that we face. They are buried in thousands of years of the church's history and tradition. Most people are completely unaware of what will be presented herein.

We cannot seek together for the solution until we first agree that there is a problem! It will take a few chapters to make us ready for *"21st Century Zerubbabels."*

We need to evaluate what some are labeling "the last reformation" in the light of our present condition. Therefore, we must reflect on today's church in light of what Scripture defines as God's purpose for our very existence.

I respectfully submit the following for your prayerful consideration:

Four things to make abundantly clear:

1. While Paul enjoyed a rich and deep relationship with the elders of the church in Ephesus (Acts 20:17-38), Chapter 4 of his Epistle was a target not yet realized even to this time. I know of no church in history that has matured to the fullness of the objective detailed in that chapter.

2. The gospel of individual salvation has displaced the gospel of the kingdom, including all of its corporate implications. (See Matthew 3:2, 4:17, 10:7, 24:14.) Please also note the priority of prayer given in Jesus' model, to praying for the kingdom *on earth as it is in heaven.*

3. The missing ingredient is the unique role of apostles. The correction of the direction of the church will require the biblical function of authentic apostles.

4. Today's apostles have themselves failed to see the problem and forthrightly address it. Instead, we have built our own houses (apostolic networks and apostolic work centers) rather than building the house of God.

Is it time for you yourselves to dwell in your paneled houses while this house [of the Lord] lies in ruins?

Now therefore thus says the Lord of hosts: Consider your ways and set your mind on what has come to you. You have sown much, but you have reaped little; you eat, but you do not have enough; you drink, but you do not have your fill; you clothe yourselves, but no one is warm; and he who earns wages has earned them to put them in a bag with holes in it.

Thus says the Lord of hosts: Consider your ways (your previous and present conduct) and how you have fared. Go up to the hill country and bring lumber and rebuild [My] house, and I will take pleasure in it and I will be glorified, says the Lord [by accepting it as done for My glory and by displaying My glory in it].[1]

---

[1] Haggai 1:4-8 AMPC

Here's a redemptive thought: I remember the parable of *the pearl of great price*:

"The kingdom of heaven is like a merchant seeking fine pearls, and upon finding one pearl of great value, he went and sold all that he had and bought it"[2]

Frankly, I am blown away by the recent discoveries that are being unearthed for my understanding. I hope and pray that your spirit bears witness with my spirit that what is presented here is worthy of our prayerful consideration. For me, it has become a "no-brainer" to sell out in order to have my hands free to receive this *pearl of great value.*

For many, it's not so easy to say or do.

"It is difficult to get a man to understand something when his salary depends upon not understanding it."[3]

"One cannot pray for God to lead into all truth when you think you already have all truth. We never change because we are never willing to hear things we have never heard that we may do things we have never done."[4]

As you consider the content of this book, please do so encouraged that God is gracious and kind, and that He provides where He guides. You will find that I am not suggesting any sudden change in direction. Rather, I believe that God will graciously guide us in wisdom on strategies individually prescribed for our individual situations. This is not a "how to" book. I purpose to leave the reader dependent upon the Holy Spirit for the application.

---

[2] Matthew 13:45-46
[3] Upton Sinclair
[4] Don Nori Sr.

The church is to be a living, vibrant demonstration of another kingdom, one known and recognized for *righteousness, peace and joy in the Holy Spirit. For he who in this way serves Christ is acceptable to God and approved by men. So then we pursue the things which make for peace and the building up of one another.*[5]

We have been church folks, not kingdom men and women. We are to be both—church folks and kingdom men and women.

We have been DOING church and postponing the kingdom to a future age. But, *kingdom* is what we are to be doing *now*. We BE the church; we DO the kingdom. Proper response to God's revealed will is His kingdom in action in and through us, *on earth as it is in heaven.* Doing God's will **is** *kingdom.* The church is the bride of Christ, always intended to be *a helper suitable for Him.*[6]

Do not let this one fact escape your notice, beloved, that with the Lord one day is like a thousand years, and a thousand years like one day. The Lord is not slow about His promise, as some count slowness, but is patient toward you, not wishing for any to perish but for all to come to repentance.[7]

As Publilius Syrus said, "It is better to learn late than never."[8]

We will invest our time during the first several chapters, discovering and acknowledging the problems we face. Most who read this book are accustomed to "church as usual," while what we consider as "usual" is well off the mark and unable to fulfill God's purpose for us in the earth. We will gradually unfold the intent of this book, to envision and instruct the church in her return to her Husband and His purposes.

---

[5] Romans 14:17-19
[6] Genesis 2:18
[7] 2 Peter 3:8-9
[8] Publilius Syrus

"The Lord would so cleanse the motive and desires of our hearts that we will seek but one thing only, and that is, His glory."[9]

---

[9] Smith Wigglesworth

Chapter 1

PROPHECY AND PURPOSE UNFULFILLED

L aunching into writing this book is among the greatest challenges of my long life. If it were not for the prompting of the Holy Spirit, I would not dare take on the many *sacred cows* that need to be challenged. Some would ask, ""Why don't you relax? Why don't you rest in peace? Why tamper with such a huge topic in this season of your life?"

As you will see as you read Chapter 2 and beyond, I will be pioneering in virgin territory, insofar as the present-day church is concerned. I do look forward to resting in peace in the perfect timing of the Lord. Meanwhile, I am resting in the peace of Jesus, and simply attempting to be obedient in faith.

"You can no longer remain unconscious where you slept before; one way or another, you are creating your future. Wake up before you find that the devils within you have done the creating."[1]

One of the challenges that increases as we age is the challenge to remain teachable. We tend to filter any new information through the storehouse of what we already believe. We tend to lean on our own understanding, rather than keeping our understanding on the altar of sacrifice.

We cannot expect to go (grow) from glory to glory by depending on our present beliefs alone. We know in part. And the very part that we do not yet know, that is trying to touch our spirits, is locked out by the closed gate of our minds. We are to:

Lean on, trust in, and be confident in the Lord with all your heart and mind and do not rely on your own insight or understanding.[2]

---

[1] Stephen I. Talbot
[2] Proverbs 3:5 AMPC

Paul briefly explained the higher way as he wrote to the church in Corinth:

As for myself, brethren, when I came to you, I did not come proclaiming to you the testimony and evidence or mystery and secret of God [concerning what He has done through Christ for the salvation of men] in lofty words of eloquence or human philosophy and wisdom; for I resolved to know nothing (to be acquainted with nothing, to make a display of the knowledge of nothing, and to be conscious of nothing) among you except Jesus Christ (the Messiah) and Him crucified.[3]

"Those who make history are those who submit to the One who orchestrates it."[4]

I certainly am laying no claim to fame, or trying to identify with another or even trying to elevate the importance of this book. I'm just saying that I wonder how Martin Luther felt as he penned and then nailed his 95 Theses on the door of All Saints' Church in Wittenberg, which resulted in the Protestant Reformation in 16th-century Europe.

Perhaps he felt a similar fear and trembling offset by the presence and urging of the Spirit within. This is a good place to be.

There are many unanswered questions, unanswered prayers, unfulfilled prophecies, and—above all—the revealed will of God has not been fulfilled. Let's begin there.

THE KINGDOM OF GOD ON EARTH

The specifics of the Lord's Prayer have been filled, time and time again, with the exception of one item: the kingdom of God has not been established *on earth as it is in heaven.*

"Your kingdom come, Your will be done on earth as it is in heaven."[5]

---

[3] 1 Corinthians 2:1-2 AMPC
[4] John r. Mott
[5] Matthew 6:10

Sound familiar? Have you ever prayed like this? Have you ever heard others pray for God's kingdom to come, His *will to be done on earth as it is in heaven?*

Many believe that heaven is somewhere else, and will be a Utopian upgrade, with streets paved with gold. Many believe the kingdom to be sometime in the future.

If that were so, why did Jesus say to the chief priests and elders of the temple, *"The kingdom of God will be taken away from you and given to a people producing the fruit of it?"[6]*

If the kingdom is someplace else, sometime later, then why did Jesus say this? It seems more logical to believe that the Israelites were stewarding the kingdom, but not doing an acceptable job of it. They were not producing the fruit of the kingdom.

If they were expected to produce kingdom fruit wouldn't that mean that the kingdom of God was in their midst?

Asked by the Pharisees when the kingdom of God would come, He replied to them by saying, "The kingdom of God does not come with signs to be observed or with visible display, nor will people say, Look! Here [it is]! or, See, [it is] there! For behold, the kingdom of God is within you [in your hearts] and among you [surrounding you].[7]

Jesus also instructed His disciples to seek first the kingdom of God. How illogical it would be to give such a high priority to something that would not become reality for thousands of years. In another context, Jesus promised, "Seek and you will find." Surely, this implies the immediate availability of the kingdom to honest seekers.

---

[6] Matthew 21:44
[7] Luke 17:20-21

CREATION WAITS EXPECTANTLY

For [even the whole] creation (all nature) waits expectantly and longs earnestly for God's sons to be made known [waits for the revealing, the disclosing of their sonship].[8]

Birth pangs continue in hurricanes, tornados, earthquakes, flooding, fires, etc., while the creation itself awaits the orderly and peaceful dominion of *the sons of the kingdom.*[9]

That nature (creation) itself will be set free from its bondage to decay and corruption [and gain an entrance] into the glorious freedom of God's children.[10]

Surely, all of creation is deceived if the sons are to be revealed somewhere else! Or else, those who believe that the kingdom is only in heaven are the ones who are deceived. Remember the prayer:

*"Your kingdom come, Your will be done **on earth** as it is in heaven."*[11]

It has always been, and remains today, that God created the earth for His kids to rule! This, on a grand scale, expresses the heart of fatherhood—preparing a place for family fruition!

*And God blessed them and said to them, "Be fruitful, multiply, and fill the earth, and subdue it [using all its vast resources in the service of God and man]; and have dominion over the fish of the sea, the birds of the air, and over every living creature that moves **upon the earth."**[12]*

---

[8] Romans 8:19 AMPC
[9] Matthew 13:38
[10] Romans 8:21 AMPC
[11] Matthew 6:10
[12] Genesis 1:28 AMPC

THE GLORY OF THE LORD

All the earth will be filled with the glory of the LORD.[13]

Surely, no generation has seen this amazing prophecy fulfilled! Let's settle in then, and prayerfully and faithfully consider the pages and chapters that follow, understanding that:

If then you have been raised with Christ [to a new life, thus sharing His resurrection from the dead], aim at and seek the [rich, eternal treasures] that are above, where Christ is, seated at the right hand of God.

And set your minds and keep them set on what is above (the higher things), not on the things that are on the earth. For [as far as this world is concerned] you have died, and your [new, real] life is hidden with Christ in God.

When Christ, Who is our life, appears, then you also will appear with Him in [the splendor of His] glory.[14]

This passage points us toward a lifestyle of being led by the Holy Spirit as *sons of God.*[15] As we so live, there will be special times when *we will appear with Him in glory* because of His work in and through us. It also points us to the ultimate consummation of all things in Christ.

CONSUMMATION OF ALL THINGS IN CHRIST

In Him we have redemption (deliverance and salvation) through His blood, the remission (forgiveness) of our offenses (shortcomings and trespasses), in accordance with the riches and the generosity of His gracious favor, which He lavished upon us in every kind of wisdom and understanding (practical insight and prudence), making known to us the mystery (secret) of His will (of His plan, of His purpose). [And it is this:] In accordance with His good pleasure (His merciful intention) which He had previously purposed and set forth in Him, [He planned] for the maturity of the

---

[13] Numbers 14:21
[14] Colossians 3:1-4 AMPC
[15] Romans 8:14

times and the climax of the ages to unify all things and head them up and consummate them in Christ, [both] things in heaven and things on the earth.[16]

Creation waits for the revealing of the sons of God. The earth will reveal the glory of God. And, there will be a consummation of all things in Christ.

None of the above will be fully realized without the administration of those who are compared with *wise master builders.*[17] Zerubbabel was appointed the master builder for the second temple in Jerusalem—a physical building where the Israelites believed God was present.

21st Century Zerubbabels are appointed to build together living stones—every stone filled with the Spirit of God—into a spiritual temple. We must face the challenges head-on, in faith, so that God's kingdom may truly be fully known *on earth as it is in heaven.*

We are God's house, God's dwelling place!

---

[16] Ephesians 1:7-10 AMPC
[17] 1 Corinthians 3:10

Chapter 2

THE ELEPHANT IN THE ROOM

Do you know the difference between a *house* and a *dwelling place*? That person down the street who is a Christian who is part of a different congregation, a different denomination, lives *in the same house* that you live! He dwells in *a different p*lace, but in the same house!

*"In My Father's **house** are many dwelling **places**; if it were not so, I would have told you; for I go to prepare **a place for you**."[1]*

ONE HOUSE; MANY DWELLING PLACES

Jesus went to prepare a special place just for you, me, and others. He returned in the Spirit to inhabit His body, the church. There is a significant link between His going and His return. Christ in us gives us our identity and placement within His body, through the unity of the Spirit.

The companion truth is that God *made us alive together with Christ, and raised us up with Him, and seated us with Him in the heavenly places in Christ Jesus.[2]*

This is among the most hidden parts of the magnificent mystery of Christ! It is illogical. We are unable to get our heads around it. But, we can believe it:

- Christ is in us, His house on earth
- We are in Christ, our house in heaven
- Heaven and earth are both included in the spiritual realm

Father's house is that one and same house, featuring as many dwelling places as there are members of His family! (We all get

---

[1] John 14:2
[2] Ephesians 2:5-6

our own room!) We all get our own place in the function of the kingdom!

- *Each one is given the manifestation of the Spirit for the common good.*[3]
- *And God has placed the members, each one of them, in the body, just as He desired.*[4]
- *We are His workmanship, created in Christ Jesus for good works, which God prepared beforehand so that we would walk in them.*[5]

OUR PLACEMENT IS TIED TO OUR PURPOSE

We are to function in our unction. That is, we are to do the works which God prepared for us; do what we do as parts of the works of the entire household!

Speaking the truth in love, we are to grow up in all aspects into Him who is the head, even Christ, from whom the whole body, being fitted and held together by what every joint supplies, according to the proper working of each individual part, causes the growth of the body for the building up of itself in love.[6]

THE ELEPHANT IN THE LIVING ROOM

The elephant in the living room is a huge handicap constantly and negatively affecting the mission of the church, which is to multiply, and fill the earth with God's glory.

The devil cannot wipe the smile off his face! The ruling principalities in every geopolitical sphere continue, decade after decade, to go unidentified and unchallenged. Powers of darkness maintain choke holds on the saints, not to mention their sentence of death upon all who are in the world. The prince of the power of the

---

[3] 1 Corinthian 12:7
[4] 1 Corinthians 12:18
[5] Ephesians 2:10
[6] Ephesians 4:15-16

air reports to the archenemy of our souls, "No problem!" The gates of hell continue to prevail against the church.

The devil's first job is to keep us from Jesus and His kingdom. His second is to keep believers divided so that they will remain unfruitful.

Don't think that your unawareness of any conflict with the demon world means that you are free from such influences. It simply means that you are temporarily in the dark concerning these matters.

Nevertheless, there is an elephant trespassing in the living room of God's house, where we are meant to do life together. Its huge influence on how we live our lives is not obvious to us, because we were born and baptized into the church under that influence. All seems normal to us. When we are born with an elephant in the room, that's the way we think it is supposed to be. We think that we all are to stay in our own rooms!

We cannot even imagine the spacious freedom that we would gain together if the elephant were no longer there. We cannot even imagine the potential interaction of the global body of Christ that will be ours when the elephant is gone.

Yes, all of us are handicapped. All believers have had the entertaining of the elephant as our primary activity, and didn't even know it! How could something so huge, which takes up so much space, be in our lives but not in our awareness?

This has been going on for nearly two thousand years! Our fathers, grandfathers, their grandfathers—generation before generation, going all the way back to the first century—have been unaware of the elephant in the living room. But, it has been there all along.

The elephant feasts and thrives on unbelief. This unbelief is caused by the darkness in the room. We've learned to navigate our places in darkness from infancy because of our failures to walk together in the light.

Many of us have our own individual victorious moments and testimonies. That is good. Jesus said that we would be *witnesses unto Him when the Holy Spirit comes upon* us.[7]

It has been my joy to lead hundreds to Christ, both by personal witness, and by crusades in India. I received the release of the Spirit within me on a Thursday evening, and led a family of four to receive Him on Friday morning. That became a way of life that has been quite fulfilling. (I fully believe that the primary purpose of the power given us by the Holy Spirit is to enable us to be His witnesses.[8])

We have had faith for some things. But, we have not had faith "*to pluck up and to break down, to destroy and to overthrow, to build and to plant.*"[9]

WE HAVE PLANTED, BUT NOT BUILT

God's words to Jeremiah have also been spoken by Paul and others—especially the words, "*to build and to plant.*"

There is an important change in this metaphor shared by Paul for our understanding:

Now he who plants and he who waters are one; but each will receive his own reward according to his own labor. For we are God's fellow workers; you are God's field, God's building.

According to the grace of God which was given to me, like a wise master builder I laid a foundation, and another is building on it. But each man must be careful how he builds on it.[10]

---

[7] Acts 1:8

[8] Much unnecessary division still exists in the church because of tongues. And few realize the greater purpose of His presence in us and with us.

[9] Jeremiah 1:10

[10] 1 Corinthians 3:8-10

Paul changed metaphors from planting to building. We have done much *planting*, but not any real building. We yet remain individuals who may be *living stones*. But, we are not *built together*. The elephant in the room will only be cast out of the way *as living stones, are being built up as a spiritual house for a holy priesthood.*[11]

We continue to perpetuate the purpose of the elephant by assembling only with likeminded people, thus adding to the schisms and breaches in the body of Christ, the household of God.

You are A CHOSEN RACE, A royal PRIESTHOOD, A HOLY NATION, A PEOPLE FOR God's OWN POSSESSION, so that you may proclaim the excellencies of Him who has called you out of darkness into His marvelous light.[12]

Yes, we have *planted*, and we have *watered*. And we have *harvested* souls. But, we have failed to be built together as a representative race, a royal priesthood, and a holy nation.

Here is the yet-to-be-realized truth concerning us:

You are no longer outsiders or aliens, but fellow-citizens with every other Christian—you belong now to the household of God. Firmly beneath you in the foundation, God's messengers and prophets, the actual foundation-stone being Jesus Christ Himself. In Him each separate piece of building, properly fitting into its neighbor, grows together into a temple consecrated to God. You are all part of this building in which God Himself lives by His Spirit.[13]

The elephant in the living room of God's house continues to keep us in our own rooms with those who are like-minded.

---

[11] 1 Peter 2:5
[12] 1 Peter 2:9
[13] Ephesians 2:19-22 AMPC

What is the elephant's name? Sectarianism.

No one can see today's temple of the Holy Spirit, for we are scattered across the land without any cohesive integrity. What is on display, for the most part, is a reflection of the world redressed in religious consumerism.

Chapter 3

DRY BONES

Ezekiel's vision of the valley of dry bones[1] is one perspective one might get when looking at Father's house from heaven's view.

The church of the New Covenant already exists. You will find it scattered across the landscape of many localities, gathering in halls and homes, each group seeking authenticity on its own, apart from the rest of the church where they live.

"*Grotesque* has come to be used as a general adjective for the strange, fantastic, ugly, incongruous, unpleasant, or disgusting, and thus is often used to describe weird shapes and distorted forms such as Halloween masks."[2]

Fantasy-masked according to the various perspectives of men, the house of God is in need of major renovation. It will take much more than plastic surgery to remove the elephant from the living room. However, it does not need the renovations perceived by still other men. If we had the vision and could take the time to see the thousands of man-made distinctives already taking up space, we would realize that it is futile to offer yet another human opinion or option.

Add-ons and missing parts combine to rob *the bride* of her ability to truly be a *helper suitable for her Husband*.[3] She cannot accurately glorify[4] (represent) Him to the world. From heaven's perspective, the *bride* is schizophrenic, having multiple

---

[1] Ezekiel 37
[2] Wikipedia
[3] Genesis 2:18; Ephesians 5:32
[4] 1 Corinthians 11:7

personalities, self-centered, and totally confused about her identity and purpose.

DISTINCTIVES GIVEN BY GOD

Distinctives themselves may come from God. But He intends for them to be contextualized within the one body, the church where we live. Whenever we identify with our distinctive(s), rather than, or in addition to, identifying with Jesus, what we are building looks grotesque from heaven's perspective. When we love our distinctives more than our family in Christ, a healing, maybe deliverance, is needed.

Unless the LORD builds the house, they labor in vain who build it.[5]

Scripture points out that the various *spirituals* (gifts) are given to the body of Christ *for the common good.*

Now there are varieties of gifts, but the same Spirit. And there are varieties of ministries, and the same Lord. There are varieties of effects, but the same God who works all things in all persons. But to each one is given the manifestation of the Spirit for the common good.[6]

We are told that, as a result of the equipping ministries, *we are no longer* (to be) *children, that we are to grow up in all aspects into Him who is the head, even Christ, from whom the whole body, being fitted and held together by what every joint supplies.*[7]

It is a huge mystery to me how we could have survived nearly two thousand years in our undone and childish condition, reading these passages many times, and yet believe that somehow we are mature and *equipped for works of service.*

I have not met many of those in the local church (the church in my geopolitical sphere) who carry *manifestations of the Spirit* for my

---

[5] Psalm 127:1
[6] I Corinthians 12:4-7
[7] Ephesians 4:11-16

good. In no way our little home groups, or our huge mega-churches, or the multitudes between these extremes have been the benefactor of all the necessary equipping ministries who make it possible to *grow up in all aspects into Christ.*

THE NEED TO KNOW IDENTITY AND PURPOSE

God's design, the blueprint for our individual lives, requires workers sent to us by God that we might mature into who we are in Christ and what is our purpose within the context of the church in our locality.

For by grace you have been saved through faith; and that not of yourselves, it is the gift of God; not as a result of works, so that no one may boast. For we are His workmanship, created in Christ Jesus for good works, which God prepared beforehand so that we would walk in them.[8]

. . . so that we would walk in them!

- Who am I? What is my *identity*?
- Where am I from? What is my *source*?
- Why am I here? What is my *purpose*?
- What can I do? What is my *potential*?
- Where am I going? What is my *destiny*?

These questions have never been fully answered. The church has never come to this kind of completeness and maturity. Our carnal minds compute maturity based upon longevity. Wrong!

We need a season—perhaps a long season—of coming into an accurate and detailed awareness of God's love for His kids, Jesus' love for His bride.   Before we dare consider first steps in renovating the dwelling place of the Most High God, we must first be prepared by Him:

---

[8] Ephesians 2:8-10

Therefore humble yourselves [demote, lower yourselves in your own estimation] under the mighty hand of God, that in due time He may exalt you, Casting the whole of your care [all your anxieties, all your worries, all your concerns, once and for all] on Him, for He cares for you affectionately and cares about you watchfully.

To Him be the dominion (power, authority, rule) forever and ever. Amen (so be it).[9]

During this process, we will increase in our spiritual vision to see the works of our own hands from His perspective. Only those who have truly humbled themselves will be able to withstand such humiliation. Only those who have truly emptied themselves will be filled with *Jesus Christ, the hope of glory.*

- *Hope does not disappoint.*
- *Wisdom* chooses a transgenerational approach.
- *Strategy* looks for youngers who trust and honor elders (in spite of our track records).
- *Integrity* insists that the elders say to the youngers, "We did not know."
- *Honesty* causes the youngers to say to the elders, "We do not know."
- *Unity* enables them together to say, "I AM knows!"

DREAMS AND VISIONS

Three years prior to God's pouring out His Spirit on all mankind, Jesus began the lifestyle discipling of those who would become the apostles of the Lamb. Interestingly, God spoke in Joel: *"your old men shall dream dreams; your young men shall see visions."*

---

[9] 1 Peter 5:6-11 AMPC

We still carry unfulfilled dreams in our hearts. We need the young 21st century Zerubbabels who are seeing the visions of what we dream.

We old men, old apostles, tried to add our apostolicity as an overlay on the divided church of the twentieth century. This activity, which continues today, only serves to further divide the church.

Among my most exciting and fulfilling experiences in these times are the younger men and women in my life. Some are one generation behind me; others are two generations behind me. Yet, in so many ways, they are in front of me, eager to *seek first the kingdom of God and His righteousness.* I love to lift them up.

I often meet young men and women who envision what I have dreamed. My joy is to undergird and encourage them in their race, their pursuit of the kingdom.

My hope and prayer is that they (you) will forsake the trappings of men and return to the ways of God.

"The wind blows (breathes) where it wills; and though you hear its sound, yet you neither know where it comes from nor where it is going. So it is with everyone who is born of the Spirit."[10]

Returning to Ezekiel's vision of the valley of dry bones, we find that, in obedience, Ezekiel prophesied:

So I prophesied as I was commanded; and as I prophesied, there was a noise, and behold, a rattling; and the bones came together, bone to its bone. And I looked, and behold, sinews were on them, and flesh grew and skin covered them; but there was no breath in them. Then He said to me, "Prophesy to the breath, prophesy, son

---

[10] John 3:8 AMPC

of man, and say to the breath, 'Thus says the Lord GOD, "Come from the four winds, O breath, and breathe on these slain, that they come to life."'" So I prophesied as He commanded me, and the breath came into them, and they came to life and stood on their feet, an exceedingly great army.[11]

I am prophesying to the dry bones. I am listening for a noise, the rattling. I dream of us all being united and strengthened by the sinew of God's strength, resilience, elasticity, power in the freedom of oneness.

We are necessarily taking the time to fully realize the problem before we can fully entertain the way forward. The following brief testimony illustrates where much of the church is today.

---

[11] Ezekiel 37:7-10

Chapter 4

LIKE A MIGHTY WIND

A greeing to shepherd a small congregation in 1973, among my first activities was to answer a call from an elderly shut-in lady. She explained that she had heard a preacher on the radio talking about the assurance of salvation. She said, "I have been in church all of my life. I received many awards for perfect attendance in Sunday school during my childhood. But, I do not know what the preacher meant by the assurance of salvation. I don't have it!"

After spending some time with her, she became confident of her relationship with Jesus, and had the assurance of her salvation. She died within days of that appointment.

The simple truth is that many church members have been taught ABOUT Jesus, but have not been brought to know Him. Knowing Jesus (NOT SIMPLY KNOWING **ABOUT** HIM) is the foundation for life in the Spirit and for being built into His household. This passage reveals the difference:

*But you did not so **learn** (NOT SIMPLY LEARN **ABOUT**) Christ! Assuming that you have really **heard Him** (NOT SIMPLY HEARD **ABOUT** HIM) and **been taught by Him** (NOT SIMPLY TAUGHT **ABOUT** HIM), as [all] Truth is in Jesus [embodied and personified in Him].*[1]

In 1968, I prepared a brochure introducing the ministry that we were about to launch. Upon reading it, a young pastor, having just graduated from Bible College, questioned me, "What do you mean when you say, 'the person of Jesus?'" He was typical of so many who had not yet realized the difference between knowing Jesus and

---

[1] Ephesians 4:20-21 AMPC. Caps are my words; bold emphasis mine.

knowing about Him. "I know about George Washington. But, I don't know him," I responded.

KNOWING JESUS IS THE FOUNDATION

Jesus, not information ABOUT Him, is the apostolic foundation of the church. The fruit of salvation and the evidence of the kingdom is: *Christ in* (all of) *you* (together is), *the hope of glory.*[2]

*For [as far as this world is concerned] you have died, and your [new, real] life is hidden with Christ in God. When **Christ**, Who is **our life**, appears, then you also will appear with Him in [the splendor of His] glory.*[3]

The Spirit of Christ has come in our flesh! This is our testimony! He promised: *The Spirit of Truth, Whom the world cannot receive (welcome, take to its heart), because it does not see Him or know and recognize Him. But you know and recognize Him, for He lives with you [constantly] and will be **in you** (the hope of glory).*

I will not leave you as orphans [comfortless, desolate, bereaved, forlorn, helpless]; I will come [back] to you. Just a little while now, and the world will not see Me anymore, but you will see Me; because I live, you will live also.[4]

Much of the church as we know it is organized, institutionalized and administrated based largely on information about Jesus. Information does not produce formation (forming Christ in us, *the hope of glory*).[5]

---

[2] Colossians 1:27 AMPC. Caps are my words.
[3] Colossians 3:3-4 AMPC
[4] John 14:17-19 AMPC
[5] Colossians 1:27; Galatians 4:19

WIND OF THE SPIRIT

"Like a Mighty Wind" by Mel Tari was first published in 1965. Millions of copies sold, translated into nineteen foreign languages, top of the national best-seller list for thirteen consecutive months: these are just some of the superlatives this remarkable book can boast. This is the powerful story of incredible miracles in Indonesia. This is the book that swept America with the reality that miracles are for today!

Those who have seen the devastation of tornados and hurricanes will agree that **wind changes everything. The wind of the Spirit changes things for good!** Our changed lives are the evidence of the wind of the Spirit.

Jesus said to Nicodemus, "The wind blows (breathes) where it wills; and though you hear its sound, yet you neither know where it comes from nor where it is going. So it is with everyone who is born of the Spirit."[6]

What could this mean? This is God's new creation, a people of flexibility, elasticity, spontaneity. They are unpredictable, unexplainable, beyond human comprehension—a totally out-of-the-box counter-culture bringing heaven to earth by the power of the Spirit.

What happened? This doesn't sound at all like the church we see today!

GOD'S DIVINE ORDER

God's order, as simple to understand as "A, B, C" and "One, two, three," has been largely ignored since even before the days of Constantine. Jesus said, *"I will build My church."*

---

[6] John 3:8 AMPC

Any architect, general contractor, or wise master builder will spell out the order for us. The process is: **(first)** *initiating and building*, **(second)** *establishing* and **(third)** *maturing or completing* the building process. God's order, simply stated by the inspired words of Paul:

*And God has appointed in the church, **first apostles, second prophets, third teachers . . .***[7]

Come to Him [then, to that] Living Stone which men tried and threw away, but which is chosen [and] precious in God's sight. [Come] and, like living stones, be yourselves built [into] a spiritual house, for a holy (dedicated, consecrated) priesthood,[8] *to offer up [those] spiritual sacrifices [that are] acceptable and pleasing to God through Jesus Christ.*[9]

We can begin right where we are without requiring anything from anyone else.

I remember one young "hippy" disciple back in the Jesus Movement. When asked how he was, he always replied, "Bubble, bubble, bubble!" This was his way of testifying to *the river of life* bubbling up within his spirit. He was evidencing the effect of the mighty wind of the Spirit.

Set your sails to catch the wind! Become unpredictable, unexplainable, beyond human comprehension. Become a living stone yielded to being built together as the Lord wills. Bear witness to the various grace gifts within your sphere. And, ask our Father to reveal His order in your midst.

---

[7] 1 Corinthians 12:28
[8] "In the New Testament no individual Christian is specifically identified as a priest. Jesus is called a priest, and the church as a whole is called a royal priesthood, but there was no particular group of priests in the New Testament Church." – Raymond Brown
[9] 1 Peter 2:4-5 AMPC

I am not recommending sudden and radical changes which would certainly scatter the sheep. Follow the wind of the Spirit using your present structures as temporary scaffolding. He will let you know when and how to retool for continuing progress.

So much of what needs adjusting is heart issues and issues of faith. Simply grasping that it is God's will for His church to present a united front in every locality, and yielding to His guidance are vital keys.

"The great Christian revolutions came not by the discovery of something that was not known before. They happen when someone takes radically something that was always there."[10]

This is beginning to happen, not everywhere, but in some places. The wind of the Spirit is beginning to move people in a direction that is closer to Him and His will for His church.

---

[10] H. Richard Niebuhr

Chapter 5
EQUIPPERS AND KINGDOM ACTIVITY

There are some encouraging signs of growing awareness among some servant-leaders in some cities and regions. At this point, those of us with a passionate commitment to see the church come together in God's purpose are almost ready to take a risk and allow ourselves to get excited, knowing that plans of the past have been dashed for premature timing, or for lack of specific vision.

It's one thing to realize and come to grips with the truth that God *gave some as apostles, and some as prophets, and some as evangelists, and some as pastors and teachers.* It is good to understand that their combined purpose is for *the equipping of the saints for the work of service, to the building up of the body of Christ.* For all the church to *attain to the unity of the faith, and of the knowledge of the Son of God, to a mature man, to the measure of the stature which belongs to the fullness of Christ* is totally mind-boggling! Who can imagine?

To date, our spiritual family, the body of Christ—is divided into thousands of denominations. Those who claim to be non-denominational are as steeped in their own defining distinctives, and consequently divided from others by some of those distinctives.

We might agree that *there is one body and one Spirit, just as also (we) were called in one hope of (our) calling; one Lord, one faith, one baptism, one God and Father of all who is over all and through all and in all.*

However, we are not *being diligent to preserve the unity of the Spirit in the bond of peace.* We are not yet ready to *walk in a manner worthy of the calling with which (we) have been called, with all humility and gentleness, with patience, showing tolerance for one another in love.*

So, when a few brethren in a city or a region actually begin to connect, perhaps for prayer or perhaps for lunch, rejoice in the Lord! This is HUGE!

TWO EXAMPLES

- "Three years ago a group of pastors and church leaders who had been building friendships and praying together sensed the Holy Spirit lead us to bring our churches together and begin the New Year worshiping Jesus Christ. This launched our first **ONE**. Today, the Body of Christ stands in need of true unity more than ever. **ONE 2016** will not only be a tremendous night of worship attended by God's presence, it has become an expression of Christ's prayer, *"That they may be one...that the world may believe that You sent Me"* (John 17:21). Followers of Christ throughout our city and county, please join us as we worship together and enter 2016 as **ONE in Christ Jesus!"** - An apostolic shepherd/teacher.

- "Over the years, I have heard so many say that you will never get the fivefold working together. 'Give it up. You are wasting your time!' Others say, 'You will never move the 90 % that have never shared their faith to share their faith.' The fruit of 2015 has proven the fivefold, God's order, can work together. And, when it does work together, people that have been Christians 10, 20, 30 and 40 years can be discipled and learn to share their faith." - An apostolic evangelist.

"God has one objective, and that is, to increase His Son. He purposes to have people come under the name of His Son and to share the life of His Son so that they become His own children. He designs to use these people for the increase of His Son in order that the personal Christ may also be the corporate Christ. For all the purposes of God are in His Son and all His works are intended to extend His Son!"[1]

"Learning to observe the whole system is difficult. Our traditional analytical skills can't help us. Analysis narrows our field of awareness and actually prevents us from seeing the total system."[2]

THE LORD REJOICES
TO SEE THE WORK BEGIN

Do not despise these small beginnings, for the LORD rejoices to see the work begin![3] These men and others are *seeds* willing to fall into the ground. *That which you sow does not come to life unless it dies; and that which you sow, you do not sow the body which is to be.*[4] It is so amazing and truly miraculous what God can do with people who are willing to take risks and step out in faith for what they believe. All of life for us is to be one experiment in obedience followed by another and another and another. We grow more and more into His image and into a greater understanding of both His purpose and His ways.

Then the angel who was speaking with me returned and roused me, as a man who is awakened from his sleep. He said to me, "What do you see?" And I said, "I see, and behold, a lampstand all of gold with its bowl on the top of it, and its seven lamps on it with seven spouts belonging to each of the lamps which are on the top of it; also two olive trees by it, one on the right side of the bowl and the other on its left side."

---

[1] Watchman Nee
[2] Margaret J. Wheatley
[3] Zachariah 4:10
[4] 1 Corinthians 15:36

Then I said to the angel who was speaking with me saying, "What are these, my lord?" So the angel who was speaking with me answered and said to me, "Do you not know what these are?" And I said, "No, my lord." Then he said to me, "This is the word of the LORD to Zerubbabel saying, 'Not by might nor by power, but by My Spirit,' says the LORD of hosts. 'What are you, O great mountain? Before Zerubbabel you will become a plain; and he will bring forth the top stone with shouts of "Grace, grace to it!"'"

What a picture of increasing insight, revelation and understanding.

The LORD rejoices to see the work begin!

The LORD REJOICES to see the plumb line in Zerubbabel's hand."[5]

Zerubbabel? Plumb line?

Be patient while being prepared. We will get there soon. Let's make an honest evaluation of the church so that we are not totally devastated by what we are reading.

---

[5] Zechariah 4:10

Chapter 6

A FRUIT-BEARING NATION

Most of our good fruit to date has been the saving and transforming of individual lives—salvation, healing, deliverance, newness of life, the renewing of our minds, etc. Who among us can complain about that? This has been the thrust of evangelicalism since early in the twentieth century.

However, the kingdom of God is to take us well-beyond our personal benefits, and include us as functional parts of His body. We are to be *a royal priesthood and holy nation.* Our oneness is essential to the purpose of God.

Jesus warned:

"Not everyone who says to Me, 'Lord, Lord,' will enter the kingdom of heaven, but he who does the will of My Father who is in heaven will enter. Many will say to Me on that day, 'Lord, Lord, did we not prophesy in Your name, and in Your name cast out demons, and in Your name perform many miracles? And then I will declare to them, 'I never knew you; DEPART FROM ME, YOU WHO PRACTICE LAWLESSNESS.'"

Jesus said to the chief priests and the elders of the people in the temple:

"The kingdom of God will be taken away from you and given to a people, producing the fruit thereof."[1]

It would be naïve and presumptuous for today's church to believe that we are qualified for what the Israelites had been disqualified.

---

[1] Matthew 21:43

Our concern is that, in the process of the developing of evangelical individualism, the gospel of the kingdom has been lost. Another gospel, "the gospel of salvation" has displaced it.

INTEGRAL SPIRITUAL GROWTH

We need to come to grips with the fact that there is no hope of spiritual maturity apart from being baptized, immersed along with one another into the body of Christ by the Holy Spirit.[2] We mature as we come to understand our specific roles, and pursue them within the context of the rest of the body of Christ. It is through "one-anothering" that God's grace is multiplied unto us.

There are spiritual pew potatoes, and spiritual couch potatoes. Sitting quietly, row-by-row in an audience, or sharing freely among those gathered in a home, listening no matter how intently, may provide information, but no true formation of Christ within and among us, *the (only) hope of glory.*[3]

There are multitudes identifying themselves with evangelicalism who have never led one person to Christ.

While appreciating the friendships and fellowship of the family of God, I was also self-motivated to *seek first the kingdom of God and His righteousness* from day one. I didn't realize at the time that I was responding to an internal awareness that God had a calling on my life. The only explanation for my motivation was the realization of the futility of my previous life in the flesh, and my profound gratitude for my deliverance. Not only did I want everyone to know my Lord, and everything that God had for me, I also wanted (and want) to be everything that I can become in Him for His kingdom purpose in the earth.

---

[2] 1 Corinthians 12:13
[3] Colossians 1:27

While rightly and submissively honoring my elders (trained in me from early childhood), my passion for the rule of God drove me to proactivity in my determination to fully serve Him and His kingdom. I have never doubted the legitimacy of my conversion or my calling. Nor have I ever chosen to backslide.

PETER, PAUL AND DON

Paul waited three years following his powerful conversion before going to Jerusalem to meet Peter and others. Then, fourteen years later, he made his second trip to meet with them. He was literally discipled by the Holy Spirit. He became my model, my mentor.

The rulers, elders, scribes, and the captain of the temple guard arrested and questioned Peter and John about the healing of the man who had been lame from his mother's womb. Grasp the significance of what they saw:

*Now as they observed the confidence of Peter and John and understood that they were uneducated and untrained men, they were amazed, and began to recognize them as having **been with Jesus**.*[4]

I learned from Peter and John that *being with Jesus* is the non-negotiable requirement for spiritual growth. Paul had testified,

*"I have been crucified with Christ; and it is no longer I who live, but **Christ lives in me**."*[5]

I believed that same reality for myself! I, Don Atkin, have been crucified with Christ; and it is no longer I who live, but Christ lives in me! Therefore, being with Christ is simply a matter of focus,

---

[4] Acts 4:13
[5] Galatians 2:20a

choosing to set my mind on Him, *on things above!*[6] Doing what I see Him doing.

Peter and John lived with Jesus for three years of personal discipling. They were able to see, hear and touch Him in His earthly body.

Paul came into the picture after Jesus was crucified, and His Spirit had been poured out on all flesh. He was radically converted via a powerful visit from Jesus on the road to Damascus. He was gloriously filled with and equipped and enabled by the indwelling Spirit of Christ, who led him into the realization of his sonship.

I, too, had a powerful visit from Jesus at age twenty-eight. I, too, have been gloriously filled with and equipped and enabled by the indwelling Spirit of Christ, who led me to realize my sonship. I am one of many sons whom God is bringing to glory.[7]

LEARN AND DISCERN

As for you, the anointing (the sacred appointment, the unction) which you received from Him abides [permanently] in you; [so] then you have no need that anyone should instruct you. But just as His anointing teaches you concerning everything and is true and is no falsehood, so you must abide in (live in, never depart from) Him [being rooted in Him, knit to Him], just as [His anointing] has taught you [to do].[8]

Living in the spiritual realm enables the discerning of spirits. We need to take heed to these inspired words from John:

B*eloved, do not put faith in every spirit, but prove (test) the spirits to discover whether they proceed from God; for many false*

---

[6] Colossians 3:2
[7] Romans 8:29; Hebrews 2:10
[8] 1 John 2:27 AMPC

*prophets have gone forth into the world. By this you may know (perceive and recognize) the Spirit of God: every spirit which acknowledges and confesses [the fact] that Jesus Christ (the Messiah) [actually] has become man and has come in the flesh is of God [has God for its source]; and every spirit which does not acknowledge and confess that **Jesus Christ has come in the flesh** [but would annul, destroy, sever, disunite Him] is not of God [does not proceed from Him]. This [non-confession] is the [spirit] of the antichrist, [of] which you heard that it was coming, and now it is already in the world.*

*Little children, you are of God [you belong to Him] and have [already] defeated and overcome them [the agents of the antichrist], because **He Who lives in you** is greater (mightier) than he who is in the world.*[9]

Take note of the emboldened words and connect them in their context, and in your understanding:

Jesus Christ has come in the flesh . . . He lives in you. This is the test in 1 John, and is also framed in 2 Corinthians:

*Examine and test and evaluate your own selves to see whether you are holding to your faith and showing the proper fruits of it. Test and prove yourselves [not Christ]. Do you not yourselves realize and know [thoroughly by an ever-increasing experience] that **Jesus Christ is in you**—unless you are [counterfeits] disapproved on trial and rejected?*[10]

This is the absolute core of the apostles' doctrinal foundation! If properly taught, we would see two results. (1) There would be a significant *exodus* from churches, and (2) there would be many conversions to (the reality) of Christ.

---

[9] 1 John 4:1-4 AMPC
[10] 2 Corinthians 13:5 AMPC

Both Jesus and Paul affirm this to be the essence of authentic Christianity.

Jesus: *"When He, the Spirit of Truth (the Truth-giving Spirit) comes, He will guide you into all the Truth (the whole, full Truth). For He will not speak His own message [on His own authority]; but He will tell whatever He hears [from the Father; He will give the message that has been given to Him], and He will announce and declare to you the things that are to come [that will happen in the future]."[11]*

Paul: *"I became a minister in accordance with the divine stewardship which was entrusted to me for you [as its object and for your benefit], to make the Word of God fully known [among you]—the mystery of which was hidden for ages and generations [from angels and men], but is now revealed to His holy people (the saints), to whom God was pleased to make known how great for the Gentiles are the riches of the glory of this mystery, which is* **Christ within and among you***, the Hope of [realizing the] glory."[12]*

So is the new creation: *"I will not leave you as orphans; I will come to you. After a little while the world will no longer see Me, but you will see Me; because I live, you will live also. In that day you will know that I am in My Father, and* **you in Me, and I in you.***"[13]*

Criteria for the proving of our individual salvation and status with God, is key to recognizing one another as fellows in the new creation, in the kingdom family of God.

Therefore from now on we recognize no one according to the flesh; even though we have known Christ according to the flesh, yet now we know Him in this way no longer. Therefore if anyone is in

---

[11] John 16:13 AMPC
[12] Colossians 1:25-27
[13] John 14:18-20

Christ he is a new creature; the old things passed away; behold, new things have come. Now all these things are from God, who reconciled us to Himself through Christ and gave us the ministry of reconciliation.[14]

The redeemed community includes all who are born of the Spirit and are giving themselves to the purpose of God in the earth. To better understand His purpose is the objective of this writing.

I appeal to you, dear reader, in the same Spirit that Zerubbabel obeyed. Will you walk with me in this journey of faith, a walk of trusting and obeying?

Moreover, the word of the Lord came to me, saying, "The hands of Zerubbabel have laid the foundations of this house; his hands shall also finish it. Then you shall know (recognize and understand) that the Lord of hosts has sent me [His messenger] to you.[15]

21st Century Zerubbabels are graced to help us divide soul from spirit and religion from reality. The two—soulish religion and spiritual reality—are so intermixed in today's church world.

Perhaps this can be made clear by considering the nature of religion as it is in one of the world's most complex religions—Hinduism.

---

[14] 2 Corinthians 5:16-18
[15] Zechariah 4:8-9 AMPC

Chapter 7

THE WAYS OF RELIGIOUS MEN

There is a vacuum, a place left empty in the heart of every individual. It is a hungry and thirsty place that constantly sucks as a baby for some yet-to-be-known nourishment that meets the demands of human life for something to worship. Like with a suckling with fingers, toes and pacifiers, there are "temporary fixes" that do not satisfy for long. But, eventually the human hunger will find a satisfactory "god" or "gods" that can be built into the very character of the persons, and become so much a part of them that many become evangelists, even apologists for their god(s). There is a plethora of options.

I remember my first time in India in 1984. On Saturday, my host took me into the city and showed me several displays on the sidewalk—chalk marks, carefully arranged rocks, and wilting flower blossoms. He explained, "This is a 'Saturday god.'" Staring blankly at us, the precious designer of this "Saturday god" once again dropped his eyes to the object of his worship on that particular day of the week.

"There is no fixed "number of deities" in Hinduism any more than a standard representation of "deity." There is, however, a popular perception stating that there are 330 million (or "33 crore") deities in Hinduism."[1]

Reincarnation is the religious or philosophical concept that the soul or spirit, after biological death, can begin a new life in a new body. This doctrine is a central tenet of the Hindu religion. Rats have free range, and often eat or destroy foods that could have warded off starvation for some individual(s). Cattle, pigs and goats roam freely through the streets.

---

[1] Wikipedia

Killing an animal, even those as undesirable as rats, would possibly wipe out a person forever. Some have somehow figured out how to breed and raise cattle that are not mystically a reincarnation of a human life. Go figure. I have no idea how we are to discern between a cow that is someone and a cow that isn't. Few East Indians eat beef. I also do not know why people cannot be reincarnated as fish, chicken or goats—which are often on the menu.

Helping a poor person to improve his situation is considered anathema. To do so could interrupt the rhythm or cycle of his or her progress toward a better life in a future life.

"Karma is a concept in Hinduism which explains causality through a system where beneficial effects are derived from past beneficial actions and harmful effects from past harmful actions, creating a system of actions and reactions throughout a soul's reincarnated lives forming a cycle of rebirth. The causality is said to be applicable not only to the material world but also to our thoughts, words, actions and actions that others do under our instructions."[2]

Consequently, the more affluent people can live next door to impoverished families, and ignore them and their obvious needs. They must leave them alone so that, in the next life, they do not need to repeat the same agonies.

"The caste system in India is a system of social stratification which has pre-modern origins, was transformed by the British Raj, and is today the basis of reservation in India. It consists of two different concepts, *varna* and *jāti*, which may be regarded as different levels of analysis of this system. *Varna* may be translated as "class," and refers to the four social classes which existed in the Vedic society, namely, Brahmins, Kshatriyas, Vaishyas and Shudras. Certain groups, now known as Dalits, were historically excluded from the

---

[2] Wikipedia

70

varna system altogether, and are still ostracised as untouchables. *Jāti* may be translated as *caste*, and refers to *birth*. The names of *jātis* are usually derived from occupations, and considered to be hereditary and endogamous."[3]

For example, there is a caste of fishermen. They—men, women and children—sleep in very small and basic tents on the beach, I've watched them working together with other families mornings, pulling their huge nets onto the beach, sorting for the fish from their overnight efforts.

Women, then carry the fish on their heads in baskets, and take some to the open-air fish market. (One can tell from quite a distance that one is getting close to the source of pungent and not-so-pleasant odors.) Other women and children go through neighborhoods, shouting, "Fish!" in their language. People buy their daily supply, for most do not have refrigeration.

24/7/365, that's life of the fisher class or caste. Children grow up with no option but to embrace that lifestyle as their own. Maybe in their next life they might be businessmen, doctors, engineers, or some other economically-successful person.

At the other extreme end of the spectrum from Hinduism, the religious spaces in some lives are very simply filled by such demented deceptions as "sex, drugs and rock-and-roll!" (There! I did it! I really dated myself!) Objects of worship can include heroes, sports teams and sports stars, movie stars, capitalism, dogmatism, etc. We could go on and on, listing anything that people worship, displacing their creator God.

The greatest object of worship in the Western world is *entertainment.* I will not take the time or space to prove or defend this statement. Given thought, I'm confident that most will agree.

---

[3] Wikipedia

Believers are not automatically exempt from the pull of this god of entertainment. Some churches use entertainment to draw and to keep people. We are constantly challenged to discipline ourselves and our children, seeking what we call "balance" in our lives.

John categorically summarized the issues:

Do not love or cherish the world or the things that are in the world. If anyone loves the world, love for the Father is not in him.

For all that is in the world—the lust of the flesh [craving for sensual gratification] and the lust of the eyes [greedy longings of the mind] and the pride of life [assurance in one's own resources or in the stability of earthly things]—these do not come from the Father but are from the world [itself].

- Lust of the flesh = passions = girls/guys

- Lust of the eyes = possessions = gold

- Pride of life = positions = glory

And the world passes away and disappears, and with it the forbidden cravings (the passionate desires, the lust) of it; but he who does the will of God and carries out His purposes in his life abides (remains) forever.[4]

IDOLATRY
AND WHERE WE PLACE OUR TRUST

I would like to share with you another "angle" on the religious worship of idols. This is about church folks, those who claim faith in Jesus Christ.

---

[4] 1 John 2:15-17 AMPC

Some people see the church as much the same. It is convenient to worship a god of our own making (or intellectual understanding). We are in control, and can decide on a moment's notice to change gods, change churches, whatever fills that religious void within.

Some are on the fringes. Still others are genuinely born again and parts of a new creation. Yet, their trust is in some aspect of their Christian life and faith—not exclusively in the Person of Christ.

How totally crushing and eternally damning it would be to hear His words, *"I never knew you."*

The present sectarianism is clearly and obviously epidemic and is evidence that multitudes are trusting in something added, or something taken away from *the simplicity that is in Christ.* Paul wrote of this concern in the second epistle to the church at Corinth:

I am afraid that, as the serpent deceived Eve by his craftiness, your minds will be led astray from the simplicity and purity of devotion to Christ.[5]

In his first letter to them, their condition could be attributed to their infancy:

Now I exhort you, brethren, by the name of our Lord Jesus Christ, that you all agree and that there be no divisions among you, but that you be made complete in the same mind and in the same judgment. For I have been informed concerning you, my brethren, by Chloe's people, that there are quarrels among you. Now I mean this, that each one of you is saying, "I am of Paul," and "I of Apollos," and "I of Cephas," and "I of Christ." Has Christ been divided? Paul was not crucified for you, was he? Or were you baptized in the name of Paul?[6]

---

[5] 2 Corinthians 11:3
[6] 1 Corinthians 1:10-13

Returning to this topic later in the letter, he emphasized in a way that explains the root problem of the present-day church:

And I, brethren, could not speak to you as to spiritual men, but as to men of flesh, as to infants in Christ. I gave you milk to drink, not solid food; for you were not yet able to receive it. Indeed, even now you are not yet able, for you are still fleshly. For since there is jealousy and strife among you, are you not fleshly, and are you not walking like mere men? For when one says, "I am of Paul," and another, "I am of Apollos," are you not mere men?[7]

This carnality is not seen as such in today's church world. We have simply copied the patterns and practices of previous generations who copied from those before them. This is all we've known. These are the traditions of our fathers, our grandfathers, and their fathers before them.

We've lost the keys to the kingdom, and we have no power against the gates of Hades. We are preoccupied with our various forms of idol worship, totally unaware that we are passing *by* rather than passing *through the narrow gate that leads to life.*[8]

As we proceed, may we come to grips with our need, our desperate need, for the unique ministry of the 21st century Zerubbabels.

We can all learn something from today's radical jihadists. We can see commitment in action with a willingness to embrace martyrdom in the name of religion.

We can also learn from the examples found in the Hebrews Hall of Faith:

They were stoned, they were sawn in two, they were tempted, they were put to death with the sword, they went about in sheepskins, in goatskins, being destitute, afflicted, ill treated (men of whom the

---

[7] 1 Corinthians 3:1-4
[8] Matthew 7:14

world was not worthy) wandering in deserts and mountains and caves and holes in the ground.

And all these, having gained approval through their faith, did not receive what was promised, because God had provided something better for us, so that apart from us they would not be made perfect.[9]

The Revelation of Jesus Christ, given to John on the Isle of Patmos, clearly defines the commitment of those who overcome:

Then I heard a loud voice in heaven, saying, "Now the salvation, and the power, and the kingdom of our God and the authority of His Christ have come, for the accuser of our brethren has been thrown down, he who accuses them before our God day and night. And they overcame him because of the blood of the Lamb and because of the word of their testimony, and they did not love their life even when faced with death.[10]

It is important that our faith in Christ be explained in such a way that others are willing to die for it. Surely, our hope for eternity is much better than any religion. Such a vision will lift us above religion and reveal to us, in us and through us a victorious lifestyle.

Deitrich Bonhoeffer rightly declared: "The call to Christ is a call to come and die."

Paul testified: *"I have been crucified with Christ [in Him I have shared His crucifixion]; it is no longer I who live, but Christ (the Messiah) lives in me; and the life I now live in the body I live by faith in (by adherence to and reliance on and complete trust in) the Son of God, Who loved me and gave Himself up for me.*[11]

---

[9] Hebrews 11:37-40
[10] Revelation 12:10-11
[11] Galatians 2:20 AMPC

"The religious spirit exalts the letter...worships knowledge... idolizes its concepts of GOD...at the expense of the leadership of the Spirit...the governance of the 'Spirit...at the expense of knowledge borne out of intimacy with the Spirit."[12]

Eugene H. Peterson, Author of The Message Bible, offers this perspective:

"I can't stand your religious meetings. I'm fed up with your conferences and conventions. I want nothing to do with your religion projects, your pretentious slogans and goals. I'm sick of your fund-raising schemes, your public relations and image making. I've had all I can take of your noisy ego-music. When was the last time you sang to me? Do you know what I want? I want justice - oceans of it. I want fairness - rivers of it. That's what I want. That's all I want."[13]

Could this actually be how our Father sees today's church?

Let's focus upon the task that is ours, to be builders of the temple in this 21st century. Let's expect the Holy Spirit to show us some important lessons from the life of Zerubbabel.

---

[12] Collin van Rooyen
[13] Amos chapter 5: 21 The Message Bible

Chapter 8
THE SPIRIT OF ZERUBBABEL

His name appears in the New Testament only in one place, in the genealogy found in Matthew, Chapter One. Apart from also being included in the genealogy in 1 Chronicles, Chapter Three, Zerubbabel is briefly mentioned in the Old Testament as part of the story told by Ezra, Nehemiah, Haggai and Zechariah. Yet, his contribution to his generation and to our heritage as 21st century Zerubbabels is invaluable.

From my point of view, it would be appropriate to ask that the spirit in Zerubbabel be realized in today's builders, even as John the Baptist was identified with the spirit of Elijah:

"It is he who will go as a forerunner before Him in the spirit and power of Elijah, TO TURN THE HEARTS OF THE FATHERS BACK TO THE CHILDREN, and the disobedient to the attitude of the righteous, so as to make ready a people prepared for the Lord."[1]

"He was NOT Elijah, but walked in the spirit and power of Elijah. He was called forth to, in that anointing, *turn the hearts of the fathers to the children, and the disobedient to the wisdom of the just, to make ready a people prepared for the Lord.* The whole purpose was *'to make ready a people prepared for the Lord.'* This was to happen through turning fathers' hearts to children, children's hearts to fathers. Just any fathers? No, it was the just, those who sought the Father—those who would deal with the disobedient and bring them to follow just wisdom."[2]

---

[1] Luke 1:17
[2] Pat Kaveny

We know that, in the same way, the Spirit who was **with** Zerubbabel is now **in** His 21st century Zerubbabels, who are called and sent to build the temple *made without human hands.*[3]

So, what may we learn from this brief historical overview of this man sent to build the second temple?

"In 538 BC, Zerubbabel, the leader of the tribe of Judah, was part of the first wave of Jewish captives to return to Jerusalem.[4] The Persian king appointed Zerubbabel as governor of Judah,[5] and right away Zerubbabel began rebuilding the temple with the help of Joshua, the high priest.[6] The first temple, built by King Solomon, had been destroyed by the Babylonians in 587 BC.[7]

"It took Zerubbabel two years to rebuild the foundation of the temple. Then construction was delayed by Samaritan settlers whose friendly overtures masked a hidden hostility.[8] As a result of the opposition to the temple construction, Persia withdrew support for the project, and for seventeen years the temple sat unfinished.[9]

"Finally, God sent the prophets Haggai and Zechariah to encourage and support Zerubbabel,[10] and the work on the second temple resumed. Four years later, in 515 BC, the temple was completed and dedicated with great fanfare.[11] The Jews also observed the Passover.[12] It's interesting that Zerubbabel is never mentioned in connection with the dedication ceremonies, nor is his name mentioned again after Ezra 5:1. For this reason, Zerubbabel's

---

[3] Acts 17:24
[4] Ezra 1:1-2
[5] Haggai 1:1
[6] Ezra 3:2-3, 8
[7] 2 Kings 25:8-10
[8] Ezra 4:1-5
[9] Ezra 4:21
[10] Ezra 5:1-2
[11] Ezra 6:16
[12] Ezra 6:19

temple is often referred to simply as the "second temple."

"It is obvious that the Lord God was pleased with Zerubbabel's efforts in returning the captives to Jerusalem, in building the second temple, and in reestablishing the temple worship.[13] With God's prompting, Haggai gave Zerubbabel a special blessing: *'On that day,' declares the LORD Almighty, 'I will take you, My servant Zerubbabel son of Shealtiel,' declares the LORD, 'and I will make you like My signet ring, for I have chosen you,' declares the LORD Almighty.'*[14]

"As the second temple was being built, there was a group of Jews in Jerusalem who were rather disappointed. Older Jews who recalled the size and grandeur of the first temple regarded Zerubbabel's temple as a poor substitute for the original. To their minds, it did not even begin to compare with the splendor of Solomon's temple. It was true that Zerubbabel's temple was built on a smaller scale and with much fewer resources. Also, Solomon's temple had housed the Ark of the Covenant, which was no longer in Israel's possession. And at the first temple's dedication, the altar had been lit by fire from heaven, and the temple had been filled with the Shekhinah; attendees at the second temple's dedication witnessed no such miracles."

- Zerubbabel was a man under authority
- Rebuilding the temple was his priority assignment
- He partnered with Joshua, the high priest
- He took two years to rebuild the foundation
- He faced opposition which stalled the project
- Support for the project was withdrawn
- The temple sat seventeen years unfinished
- Finally, God sent prophets to encourage and support him
- Work resumed on the second temple

---

[13] Ezra 3:10
[14] Haggai 2:23

- The temple was completed and dedicated four years later
- Zerubbabel invested twenty-three years from beginning to completion
- Zerubbabel's name was not mentioned in the dedication
- Some were disappointed that the temple was not like Solomon's
- Heaven's miraculous fire did not attend the dedication

21st century Zerubbabels should take to heart all of these lessons. Our knowing that we are appointed and sent is the foundation of our own security, not to be victimized by the enemy of our souls. We are very likely initiating a multigenerational project. The quiet affirmation in our hearts from our Father is all the evidence that we need to secure us in His plan for us.

Zerubbabel received this affirmation from God through the prophet[15] Haggai:

"On that day," declares the LORD Almighty, *"I will take you, my servant Zerubbabel son of Shealtiel," declares the LORD, '"and I will make you like my signet ring,[16] for I have chosen you,"* declares the LORD Almighty."

As a type of Christ, Zerubbabel was promised the authority of Father God. Jesus would later say, *"If you had known Me, you would have known Him and have seen Him (the Father.)"[17]* We, too, as sons of God, are promised that we will reveal the Father.

Haggai also prophesied that the second temple would one day have a magnificence to outshine the glory of the first. Haggai's word was fulfilled 500 years later when Jesus Christ arrived on the scene. Zerubbabel's temple was not as outwardly impressive as

---

[15] At that time, God spoke to the fathers in the prophets; today, each of us has bold access into the holy of holies, through Jesus. Hebrews 1:1-2; 4:16

[16] Ancient kings used signet rings to designate authority, honor, or ownership.

[17] John 14:7

Solomon's, but it had a greater glory: the Messiah Himself walked the courts of the temple that Zerubbabel built.

Hollywood's glitz and glamour attract and stimulate the flesh. Here is how God directs women to properly model the bride of Christ:

Your adornment must not be merely external—braiding the hair, and wearing gold jewelry, or putting on dresses; ⁴ but let it be the hidden person of the heart, with the imperishable quality of a gentle and quiet spirit, which is precious in the sight of God.[18]

Let us also be encouraged by the Lord's words to Zerubbabel, spoken through Zechariah:

"This is the word of the LORD to Zerubbabel saying, 'Not by might nor by power, but by My Spirit,' says the LORD of hosts. 'What are you, O great mountain? Before Zerubbabel you will become a plain; and he will bring forth the top stone with shouts of "Grace, grace to it!"'"

Also the word of the LORD came to me, saying, "The hands of Zerubbabel have laid the foundation of this house, and his hands will finish it. Then you will know that the LORD of hosts has sent me to you. For who has despised the day of small things? But these seven will be glad when they see the plumb line in the hand of Zerubbabel—these are the eyes of the LORD which range to and fro throughout the earth."[19]

---

[18] 1 Peter 3:3-4
[19] Zechariah 4:6-10

Chapter 9
THE TEMPLE AND THE TOP STONE

Zerubbabel was the architect for the building of the second temple. Not only did he lay the foundation, he finished the temple. And, not only did he finish it, he brought forth the capstone!

"The hands of Zerubbabel have laid the foundation of this house, his hands will finish it, and he will bring forth the top stone with shouts of "Grace, grace to it!"

The distinct honor of bringing forth the top stone is a part of apostolic grace. We can only imagine the thrill of seeing the temple finished by Zerubbabel through such grace! *"Grace, grace to it!"*

THE MASTER BUILDER

The master builder of any project oversees the process from beginning to end. The same grace that initiates and lays the foundation facilitates and coordinates the applications of all equipping graces. As these truths apply to the church, the apostles' role continues until the elders of the city or region are appointed and committed to the grace of God.[1]

Perhaps this has been part of the failure of contemporary apostolic efforts. Zerubbabel was much more than an occasional guest speaker with conferences, a down-line and a mailing list.

Do not be offended. There is no condemnation. I've been there and done that! We have lots of company! Please allow the Holy Spirit to make application for you. Let's get past the past and look

---
[1] Acts 14:23

into the future with renewed faith. We have not yet exhausted the number of new beginnings available in God's grace!

We have not been sent to build networks of like-minded people (more denominations). We are called and sent to reveal the heart of Jesus to His followers as we co-labor with Him, as He builds His (one) church in every locality.

Rather than evangelists drawing large crowds to an event, this building assignment begins with building trust relationships within the bonds of love with those who are already church leaders in our communities.

Zerubbabel was not just building for a few of the people. He was building for all of God's people. All of God's people, all who are included in the new creation, are *living stones*, and are to be built together into God's house. And God's house in every locality is to be built together.

And coming to Him as to a living stone which has been rejected by men, but is choice and precious in the sight of God, you also, as living stones, are being built up as a spiritual house for a holy priesthood, to offer up spiritual sacrifices acceptable to God through Jesus Christ.[2]

GOD'S LIFE IN GOD'S HOUSE

This metaphor comes to life as the Spirit of God begins to knit the hearts of His people together into the dwelling place of God, His house of *living stones* on earth. We begin to see and grasp that Jesus is truly (1) the foundation, (2) the cornerstone, (3) the indwelling life in each living stone, and finally (4) *the top stone* (also known as *the gable stone*, or *the capstone*).

---

[2] 1 Peter 2: 4-5

Father's life permeates every fiber of every living stone built together as His house—from foundation to capstone. His household is His house; His house is His household.

Zerubbabel included many people in the building process. Yet, he was recognized as the builder of the temple, much like today's architects and general contractors.

Would it be fair to state that Zerubbabel was an Old Testament *type* of an apostolic builder, Jesus was and is the *prototype*—the Pattern Son, the Firstborn among many apostles—that Paul was an *antetype*, an earlier pattern from whom we may learn? It is obvious that:

- Zerubbabel was led by the Holy Spirit
- Christ was the embodiment of the Holy Spirit
- Paul was filled with the Holy Spirit
- The new creation church is now the embodiment of the Holy Spirit

Paul, sharing as he was inspired to write by the Spirit:

Do you not know and understand that you [the church] are the temple of God, and that the Spirit of God dwells [permanently] in you [collectively and individually]? If anyone destroys the temple of God [corrupting it with false doctrine], God will destroy the destroyer; for the temple of God is holy (sacred), and that is what you are.

A LIFE-OR-DEATH TRUTH

A huge doctrinal failure has been to affirm people's faith by our silence. We have not dealt with the specificity that Jesus, demonstrated in His conversation with Nicodemus:

Now there was a certain man among the Pharisees named Nicodemus, a ruler (a leader, an authority) among the Jews, who came to Jesus at night and said to Him, "Rabbi, we know and are certain that You have come from God [as] a Teacher; for no one can do these signs (these wonderworks, these miracles—and produce the proofs) that You do unless God is with him."

Jesus answered him, "I assure you, most solemnly I tell you, that unless a person is born again (anew, from above), he cannot ever see (know, be acquainted with, and experience) the kingdom of God."

Nicodemus said to Him, "How can a man be born when he is old? Can he enter his mother's womb again and be born?"

Jesus answered, "I assure you, most solemnly I tell you, unless a man is born of water and [even] the Spirit, he cannot [ever] enter the kingdom of God. What is born of [from] the flesh is flesh [of the physical is physical]; and what is born of the Spirit is spirit. Marvel not [do not be surprised, astonished] at My telling you, You must all be born anew (from above)."³

"*I most solemnly tell you!*" I appreciate this amplification. It is totally irrational to bring people into the church but not into the kingdom. It really isn't possible. Those who are born of the Spirit make up the true church, the new creation, sons and daughters of the kingdom on earth. Integrity demands full disclosure.

I cannot imagine what it would be like to have Jesus ask, "Why did you not tell them? Why did you mislead them by your silence?"

Prevailing religious systems have allowed multitudes to be parts of church activities, wrongly believing that their attendance and financial support qualify them for heaven. They have been content hearing about Jesus and a future kingdom in heaven. They are the dry bones in Ezekiel's vision.

In an earlier chapter, we considered Ezekiel's vision of the valley of dry bones to be an apt description of the church today. Spiritually, the earth remains a vast and dry land with dry bones strewn across it, with temple stones scattered in little groups here and there.

---

³ John 3:1-7 AMPC

THE TEMPLE HAS NEVER BEEN COMPLETED!

The Capstone has never been set, because the living stones were never built together! You can't set the Capstone on living stones scattered among the dry bones across the valley! Can you imagine what a challenge it would be in a city with hundreds of local church expressions to determine on which one to place the capstone?

It has been almost two thousand years since *the Holy Spirit was poured out on all flesh.*[4] And history offers us no suitable model to which we can point. There has never been a generation in the earth since the first generation that could begin at "zero." The Epistles make it clear. So do the letters dictated by John to the seven churches in Asia.

These seven churches, as well as the recipients of the Epistles, had some things going for them that we have lost.

- Each one constituted a singular expression within its locality.

- The (singular) church in each place was served by God-appointed apostolic messengers. Each of the seven churches was addressed by Jesus in this manner: *"To the angel (messenger) of the assembly (church) in . . ."*[5]

Allow me to repeat the words given by the Holy Spirit to the people of God many generations ago. They are apt and fitting for our time:

Therefore, as the Holy Spirit says: Today, if you will hear His voice, do not harden your hearts, as [happened] in the rebellion [of Israel] and their provocation and embitterment [of Me] in the day of testing in the wilderness, where your fathers tried [My

---

[4] Joel 2:28; Acts 2:17
[5] Revelation 2:1, 8, 12, 18; 3:1, 7, 14 AMPC

patience] and tested [My forbearance] and found I stood their test, and they saw My works for forty years.

And so I was provoked (displeased and sorely grieved) with that generation, and said, "They always err and are led astray in their hearts, and they have not perceived or recognized My ways and become progressively better and more experimentally and intimately acquainted with them." Accordingly, I swore in My wrath and indignation, "They shall not enter into My rest."[6]

Let me repeat Jesus' words to the chief priests and elders in the temple: *"The kingdom of God will be taken away from you and given to a people, producing the fruit thereof."[7]*

Lest we also hear those dreadful words, please bear with me in the remaining chapters. May God's grace grant us eyes to see and ears to hear. In particular, I am hoping and praying for 21st century Zerubbabels to come forth in the grace and love of the Apostle and High Priest of our confession, to graciously, patiently and tenaciously move among us as builders of His house.

Adam was never God's "Plan A!" Israel was never God's "Plan A!" He has invested His only begotten Son, the firstborn of many brothers, in a new creation. This is His "Plan A!" There is no "Plan B."

This is not something to be lightly taken! This topic deserves our highest priority for prayerful consideration and dialogue!

Could we be the generation to restore a vision to the church of God's kingdom on earth as it is in heaven? I have a deep and profound peace and excitement in my spirit as I write these words. I have every reason to believe that it comes by way of the oneness, the union of my spirit with the Spirit of Jesus.

---

[6] Hebrews 3:7-11 AMPC
[7] Matthew 21:43

We will never gain the faith needed for the church to turn around if we focus on the past. We can't change it. We can only repent on behalf of ourselves. We can only be who we are in Jesus and do what He leads and enables us to do.

This is too big for any of us. Yet, together with God, all things are possible.

Paul's words come to mind:

I do not consider, brethren, that I have captured and made it my own [yet]; but one thing I do [it is my one aspiration]: forgetting what lies behind and straining forward to what lies ahead, I press on toward the goal to win the [supreme and heavenly] prize to which God in Christ Jesus is calling us upward.[8]

I'm in! Through the grace of God, I see myself as a 21st century Zerubbabel. I'm ready to embrace realities, love God and the brethren, and join myself with you in the Spirit of the Bridegroom.

We possess this precious treasure [the divine Light of the Gospel] in [frail, human] vessels of earth, that the grandeur and exceeding greatness of the power may be shown to be from God and not from ourselves.[9]

"We cannot solve our problems with the same thinking we used when we created them."[10]

21st century Zerubbabels are graced with a biblical worldview and righteous values that point back to Jesus' words,

"God so loved the world . . ."

---

[8] Philippians 3:13-14 AMPC
[9] 2 Corinthians 4:7 AMPC
[10] Albert Einstein

Chapter 10

DIVINE TREASURES IN EARTHEN VESSELS

M uch of what we have been taught about gifts is so mechanical and doctrinal (and often divisive) that we put severe boundaries around the boundless beauty of God. We need to realize that there are supernatural graces attending such divine treasures that are meant to bless His awaiting creation[1] through the sons and daughters of the kingdom.

The 1st century church did not receive a doctrine and then seek the gifts of the Spirit. No. They received the supernatural outpouring without previous instruction. The 21st century church receives doctrines, and many never receive the gifts. Too many live only by understanding, and thereby miss the grace and gifts intended to be experienced and exercised.

We should not think of study and intellectual pursuit as wrong. We are to honor those who pay the price of disciplined effort in order to add resources and skills to their capacities. But, all of that needs to be subject and subservient to the leading and enabling of the Holy Spirit. We need to heed:

Trust in the Lord with all you heart and do not lean on your own understanding. In all your ways acknowledge Him, and He will make your paths straight.[2]

Faith comes from hearing Him. Having faith in what Jesus said about us releases us into the boundless freedom of His Spirit. He said, *"The wind blows where it wishes and you hear the sound of*

---

[1] Romans 8:19
[2] Proverbs 3:5-6

it, but do not know where it comes from and where it is going; so is everyone who is born of the Spirit."[3]

AN ENVIRONMENT OF FREEDOM

If we can believe this about ourselves, we will be able to believe it for and on behalf of others. If we can do this for ourselves, then we should be open to affirm the same realities in and among our brothers and sisters in Christ. Abiding with faith, hope and love, enables us to embrace our fellow-workers in the kingdom with a level of honor and freedom that will also free others to be themselves in Christ.

Danny Silk, senior management pastor at Bethel Church in Redding, California, says, "We have much to learn about how to steward an environment of freedom."[4]

We choose between two laws. There are only two. And they cannot be intermixed:

1. *The law of sin and death, or*
2. *The law of the Spirit of life in Christ Jesus.[5]*

When we live by *the law of the Spirit of life in Christ Jesus,* we embrace all whom He embraces, without prejudice. We become fellow-workers with Him and with one another. The gifts within us and others become divine treasures in the realm of our own realities. And our eyes are no longer upon earthen vessels—our own or others. Our vision is elevated to the throne of grace where we abide with Christ, and with one another, in God.

"Few things overwhelm me more than an authentic display of the grace of God. Whenever the presence of God enables a person to

---

[3] John 3:8
[4] This is an excerpt from the Preface of Danny's book, "Culture of Honor."
[5] Romans 8:2

become free from lifelong issues, you can't help but be amazed at such a wonderful Savior. But grace goes beyond healing from the past; it also launches us into our divine destinies."[6]

AMAZING GRACE

Grace is built into our individual, unique, one-of-a-kind DNA. Like fingerprints, there is only one of me. There is only one of you! No one else in the family of God has the same DNA. No one else has the same spiritual DNA. We can be positively identified in the natural realm by our natural DNA. We can also be positively identified in the spiritual realm by our spiritual DNA.

Therefore, no one else can take our place, fill our shoes, or answer to our personal call to our personal divine destiny. One-size-fits-all has no place in the kingdom of God. Our Great Shepherd calls each of us by our name. We hear Him and follow, because we *know His voice.*[7]

It is when we are called together within the limiting context of human institutionalism that we automatically invoke severe restrictions upon the Wind of heaven, and upon our responses. It is no longer legitimate for us to simply put our sails up to be blown at God's discretion. It is in that bound and frustrating condition that we are re-humanized to titles, positions, job descriptions that fit the institution—the Babylonian perceptions of church leadership.

Some who are known as pastors are really apostles, some are really prophets, some are teachers, some are administrators, some are really managers, some are leaders, and some are really evangelists. All are undoubtedly combinations of some of the above. Some are indeed *shepherds*, a more descriptive translation for function than *pastor.*

---

[6] Bill Johnson
[7] John 10:4

There is no end to the plethora of possible combinations. Not only are their numerous *charisms*,[8] there are also numerous *measures*. Each one's grace is measured according to the gift.

To each one of us grace was given according to the measure of Christ's gift.[9]

LEARNING CORPORIETY

The practical ramifications of this truth include that we do not have grace to fill another's shoes. Such attempts are made by way of flesh and tradition.

No one will inherit or take over my ministry. We are grooming young men and women for their unique calling. They have their own baton and race to run. When I am done, my race will be over!

The difficulties inherent in this statement exist by human invention. They are present because of what men have built by Babylonian design. Integrity requires Holy Spirit-led strategies of transition so that God is honored and His people are preserved.

Knowing and staying within the boundaries of God's assignment(s), and eagerly embracing the grace upon and gifts in others, releases the Jesus Spirit to guide us in corporeity.

And then there is the matter of spheres:

We will not boast beyond our legitimate province and proper limit, but will keep within the limits [of our commission which] God has allotted us as our measuring line and which reaches and includes even you.[10]

---

[8] Spiritual gifts
[9] Ephesians 4:7
[10] 2 Corinthians 10:13 AMPC

94

All should be considered on the basis of reality functions for a more accurate understanding of terms.[11] The inaccurate applications of titles and offices limit the church to what we can grasp with our natural minds.

Constraining spiritual truth into human language does a disservice to the eternal overview of any said truth. *We have these treasures in earthen vessels* and they (the treasures) were never intended to be imprisoned by earthen thinking and expression.

I have strength for all things in Christ Who empowers me [I am ready for anything and equal to anything through Him Who infuses inner strength into me; I am self-sufficient in Christ's sufficiency].[12]

It is enough that we receive persons because we see Jesus in them, and/or hear Jesus through them. Let's not limit one another by our own unbelief and judgments—unbelief that causes us to be insecure about anything that we cannot understand and control.

"The idea of a life-sharing community which is much more than a human association of the like-minded, a mutual insurance of common interest, and more too than the sum of its several parts and members, is essential to Christianity."[13]

THE GOVERNMENT OF DIVINE PEACE

The peace of God upon others is evidence that they are probably under His authority. Isaiah made a huge, all-encompassing statement of truth:

---

[11] This is another reason why judgments, corrections and disciplines should be address locally, within a person's authorized sphere. 1Timothy 5:19-20
[12] Philippians 4:13 AMPC
[13] R. E. O. White

Of the increase of His government and of peace there shall be no end, upon the throne of David and over his kingdom, to establish it and to uphold it with justice and with righteousness from the [latter] time forth, even forevermore. The zeal of the Lord of hosts will perform this.[14]

We have found in our life experiences that, when peace is absent, we need to find out where we are missing the government (kingdom) of God. We find, we adjust, and the peace of God returns. And much of that has nothing to do with present circumstances.

Let the peace of Christ rule in your hearts, remembering that as members of the same body you are called to live in harmony, and never forget to be thankful for what God has done for you.[15]

"Much of what we face can't be deterred, prevented or even predicted. Thus we need to become resilient."[16]

And God's peace [shall be yours, that tranquil state of a soul assured of its salvation through Christ, and so fearing nothing from God and being content with its earthly lot of whatever sort that is, that peace] which transcends all understanding shall garrison and mount guard over your hearts and minds in Christ Jesus.[17]

We have found that an accurate understanding of these contributes to living in peace:

- Our gift mix
- Our measures of grace
- The boundaries of our placement

---

[14] Isaiah 9:7 AMPC
[15] Colossians 3:15 J. B. Phillips
[16] Joshua Cooper Ramo
[17] Philippians 4:7 AMPC

- The boundaries of our sphere

The proper stewarding of our divine treasures, and functioning within our allotment, are evidences of being yoked with Jesus in the expressions of His continuing ministry *on earth as it is in heaven*. He promised:

Come to Me, all you who labor and are heavy-laden and overburdened, and I will cause you to rest. [I will cause and relieve and refresh your souls.] Take My yoke upon you and learn of Me, for I am gentle (meek) and humble (lowly) in heart, and you will find rest (relief and ease and refreshment and recreation and blessed quiet) for your souls. For My yoke is wholesome (useful, good—not harsh, hard, sharp, or pressing, but comfortable, gracious, and pleasant), and My burden is light and easy to be borne. [18]

What we have freely received we can freely give. Those who receive us receive the God of the government (kingdom) and therefore, the government of God. Truly, the kingdom has come near them. Jesus said,

"Whatever city or village you enter, inquire who is worthy in it, and stay at his house until you leave that city. As you enter the house, give it your greeting. If the house is worthy, give it your blessing of peace. But if it is not worthy, take back your blessing of peace." [19]

THE BLESSING IS IN THE RECEIVING

Near the end of this chapter in Matthew's gospel, Jesus also said,

---

[18] Matthew 11:28-30 AMPC
[19] Matthew 10:11-13

"He who receives you receives Me, and he who receives Me receives Him who sent Me. He who receives a prophet in the name of a prophet shall receive a prophet's reward.[20]

Be reminded that the New Testament church had not yet been born; and neither had the Holy Spirit been poured out. God still *spoke to the fathers in the prophets.*[21] It was important for people to receive prophets in the name of prophets—according to who they were—God's spokesmen.

However that system, necessary for God's communication to men of flesh, was instantly upgraded with the outpouring of the Holy Spirit on all flesh on the day of Pentecost. *In these last days (God) has spoken to us in His Son.*[22]

The field of service was greatly multiplied and magnified with the advent of a new creation.

It is important for people to receive us for who we are in Christ. That is their responsibility—not something that we should expect or demand. It is something that they realize because of their submission to the governance of the Spirit.

Once again, Jesus referred to the prophet, being God's primary messengers before Pentecost, *"A prophet is not without honor except in his hometown and in his own household."*[23] Familiarity does not breed respect! Those who receive us for who we are in Christ receive our blessing of peace, bearing witness to the governmental order of God in their own spirits.

---

[20] Matthew 10:40-41a
[21] Hebrews 1:1
[22] Hebrews 1:2
[23] Matthew 13:57

Chapter 11

GIFT MIX AND SPRITUAL DNA

I t is important that we righteously impart the grace of God according to who we are in Christ. Many still look to the prophets for words from God, even though they claim to have received the Spirit of His Son.

God, after He spoke long ago to the fathers in the prophets in many portions and in many ways, in these last days has spoken to us in His Son, whom He appointed heir of all things, through whom also He made the world.[1]

Here we are, two thousand years after the most significant change in all of history,[2] and some are still trying to hear God through the prophets. Jesus, in whom God speaks, spoke strong words to some who had charismatic experiences and were relying on them as their ticket to heaven:

"Many will say to Me on that day, 'Lord, Lord, did we not prophesy in Your name, and in Your name cast out demons, and in Your name do many miracles?' And I will declare to them, 'I never knew you; DEPART FROM ME, YOU WHO PRACTICE LAWLESSNESS.'"[3]

How absolutely crushing, how emotionally devastating, and how eternally damning it would be to face our King in His kingdom, have Him look deeply into our eyes, and with tears of caring say, *"I never knew you."*

---

[1] Hebrews 1:1-2

[2] Pentecost A.D. 33 marked the beginning of a new creation and the New Covenant church.

[3] Matthew 7:22-23

This is not His will for anyone. It is the fruit of those who preemptively override His will with their independence.

Knowing Jesus, and having Him speak to us for the Father, is a core value of authentic Christianity. Wanting His disciples to know and understand the transition from the Mosaic dispensation to life in the Spirit, He said to them,

"I have still many things to say to you, but you are not able to bear them or to take them upon you or to grasp them now.

"But when He, the Spirit of Truth (the Truth-giving Spirit) comes, He will guide you into all the Truth (the whole, full Truth). For He will not speak His own message [on His own authority]; but He will tell whatever He hears [from the Father; He will give the message that has been given to Him], and He will announce and declare to you the things that are to come [that will happen in the future].

He will honor and glorify Me, because He will take of (receive, draw upon) what is Mine and will reveal (declare, disclose, transmit) it to you."[4]

This is not to deny or to quench the Holy Spirit ministries through prophets and those with gifts of prophecy. It is simply a necessary clarification which points us back to our relationship with our Lord. Life in the new creation is as different from natural life as the heavens are from the earth. Here is our privilege:

The anointing (the sacred appointment, the unction) which you received from Him abides [permanently] in you; [so] then you have no need that anyone should instruct you. But just as His anointing teaches you concerning everything and is true and is no falsehood, so you must abide in (live in, never depart from) Him [being rooted in Him, knit to Him], just as [His anointing] has taught you [to do].[5]

---

[4] John 16:12-14 AMPC
[5] 1 John 2:27 AMPC

The receiving of the Spirit might be called "the cocoon ministry." In the natural, fuzzy worms develop into beautiful butterflies in cocoons. In the spiritual, baby believers develop into sons of God within the cocoon ministry, the equipping ministry provided by our Father for His kids.

THE PRIMARY OBJECTIVE

The primary objective of the equipping graces—*apostles, prophets, evangelists and shepherds and teachers*[6]— is to bring the saints to a place of mature sonship where they are led by the Spirit of God. *For all who are led by the Spirit of God are sons of God.*[7]

What follows is my "invention" of a way to explain how gift mixes may work. Please keep in mind that no one of us can be labeled according to the following scheme. Remember that our lives, and therefore our ministries, are like the wind. The wind comes from various directions, and at various speeds. A breeze can cool the body on a hot day. A hurricane can level a city in a few moments.

So, take all of this with a grain of salt, asking the Spirit to imprint within your spirit what He wants you to retain.

There are four lists:

Romans 12:6-8 – These are often defined as motivational gifts
1. Prophecy
2. Serving
3. Teaching
4. Exhorting
5. Giving
6. Leading
7. Mercy

---

[6] Ephesians 4:11
[7] Romans 8:14

1 Corinthians 12:8-10 – These are manifestations of the Spirit
1. Word of wisdom
2. Word of Knowledge
3. Faith
4. Healings
5. Miracles
6. Prophecy
7. Discerning spirits
8. Tongues
9. Interpretation of Tongues

1 Corinthians 12:28 – These define God's order
1. Apostles
2. Prophets
3. Teachers
4. Miracles
5. Gifts of healing
6. Helps
7. Administrations
8. Tongues

Ephesians 4:11 – These are graces that are to equip the saints
1. Apostles
2. Prophets
3. Evangelists
4. Pastors
5. Teachers

For the purpose of understanding, let's say that your DNA is 7474:

- Your motivational gift is Mercy – 7
- Your spiritual gift is Healing – 4
- Your place of order is Administration – 7
- Your equipping grace is Pastor – 4

Again, CAUTION! This is such a flawed over-generalization! We have no way to translate measures and spheres into human conclusions.

Gifts themselves range from low to high. Two people may have what by definition seem to be similar DNAs. However, a teacher with a high teaching gift walks, talks, eats and sleeps to teach, while another is *apt to teach* part of his elding (shepherding) ministry.

Because of the failure of the church to receive the foundational ministries of the apostles and prophets, people with high teaching gifts combined with the motivational gift of leadership have built significant congregations, networks, and even denominations on the strength of their particular DNA which may be: 6335.

Motivation: Leader (6)
Manifestation: Faith (3)
God's Order: Teacher (3)
Equipping: Teacher (5)

Bottom line: *We have been crucified with Christ! Our lives are hidden in Him. When He is revealed, we will be revealed with Him in glory.*[8]

The mature, glory-revealing function of our various gift mixes must be understood within the context of the entire local body.

---

[8] Galatians 2:20; Colossians 3:3-4

Chapter 12
ABOUT PROPHETS AND TEACHERS

What follows is in no way a full description of the breadth or depth of the ministries of prophets or teachers. This chapter is about the particular roles they play in the building of the church.

Because my last name begins with "A" I was almost always assigned a seat in the front row during my school years. I was also often first in line. Being first in line was not an indication that I was more important or of greater value. It was merely a matter of order.

So it is with Paul's acknowledgement of this order:

God has appointed in the church, first apostles, second prophets, third teachers[1]

I believe that God has used the wisdom of Solomon to give us a very short and to the point explanation of these three priority roles:

Through skillful and godly Wisdom is a house (a life, a home, a family) built, and by understanding it is established [on a sound and good foundation], and by knowledge shall its chambers [of every area] be filled with all precious and pleasant riches.[2]

1. By **wisdom** *{FIRST: APOSTLES}* a house is **built**
2. By **understanding** *{SECOND: PROPHETS}* it is **established**
3. By **knowledge** *{THIRD: TEACHERS}* the rooms are **filled** with all precious and pleasant riches

---

[1] 1 Corinthians 12:28
[2] Proverbs 24:3-4 AMPC

I planted, Apollos watered, but God gave the increase.

Very little detail about prophets is offered in the Epistles. But, a little digging around, a little research leads me to believe that Apollos was very likely a prophet. He is described by some as an apologist, and by others as an excellent preacher.

Paul said it clearly: *"I laid a foundation, and another is building upon it."*

Establishing the church with understanding is foundational to God's purpose.

1. Apostles **build the church** with **wisdom**
2. Prophets **establish the church** with **understanding**
3. Teachers **fill the church** with **knowledge**

In the wisdom of God, He did not put these functions in easily definable boxes. Rather, the writers were inspired to emphasize relationships and function in order to preserve the intended organic nature of the body.

GOD HAS ONLY ONE HOUSE

Take note that all three special graces are building the same house! Today, many prophets and teachers are building their own houses (ministries), and the house of God is not established (through the grace of understanding) or filled (through the grace of knowledge).

In comforting His disciples during a conversation about His leaving, Jesus began by offering this analogy, this metaphor:

"In My Father's house are many dwelling places; if it were not so, I would have told you; for I go to prepare a place for you."[3]

---

[3] John 14:2

That apostolic grace of wisdom and revelation actually lifts and releases the other graces to greater effectiveness and fruitfulness, by placing them with specificity in their distinctive roles in God's order.

One house; many dwelling places; and one specific place for you!

- *We (Apollos and Paul) are God's fellow workers; you are God's building.*[4]

- *You are being built together into a dwelling of God in the Spirit.*[5]

- *For we are His workmanship, created in Christ Jesus for good works, which God has prepared beforehand so that we would walk in them.*[6]

- *To each one is given the manifestation of the Spirit for the common good.*[7]

- *God has placed the members, each one of them, in the body, just as He desired.*[8]

With the outpouring of the Holy Spirit and the consequential birthing of the New Covenant Church of Jesus Christ, the prophet became one part of a variety of equippers who are together graced for *the equipping the saints for the work of service.*

The unique role of the New Covenant prophet is to *establish the church in understanding of the apostles' teaching* to which the

---

[4] 1 Corinthians 3:9
[5] Ephesians 2:22
[6] Ephesians 2:20
[7] 1 Corinthians 12:7
[8] 1 Corinthians 12:18

believers are to *continually devote* themselves. Apostles, as wise master builders, lay the foundation of Christ. Prophets share in the foundational work by bringing understanding to the church about the foundation, the substance of apostolic teaching. Teachers, then, are to add comprehensive details that build upon the understanding that prophets bring, filling out the apostolic doctrines of the church to the functional fruition of God's purpose in the church.

Many believers, not realizing that the role of prophets changed with the coming of the New Covenant, are still listening for what the prophets are saying about 2016. Even cursory investigation will confirm that various prophets do not agree on much. The primary reason for what I will call "pseudo-prophetic confusion" is the lack of connection between apostles and prophets. The prophetic work of establishing the church is to be rooted in the apostolic foundation.

This is not a conscious and/or intentional error on the part of prophets. There has been no model, pattern or example for them to understand this.

It is my observation that some prophets eagerly want the church to be established in understanding. However, lacking the right kind of connection with apostles, and being unaware of that priority, leaves them to determine for themselves what they want the church to understand. I will give you two specific examples:

One prophet has focused for years on trying to make the church understand the work and realm of the Holy Spirit. Everything that he writes gives some expression of life in the Spirit. Good stuff, and quite helpful for many. However, it does not connect with God's order or purpose. Consequently, there is very little kingdom fruit, and his ministry cycles over the same ground, year after year.

The other prophet, with a high teaching gift, labors selflessly and endlessly out of his authentic devotion to God and His people. He is focused in two areas—establishing the church in understanding between law and grace, the Old Covenant and the new Covenant, and concerns about abuses of authority. He does not believe that the church will ever see authentic apostles in full operation, or the church coming into unity. He has a good revelation of the central place of relationships, but focuses upon relating with likeminded people.

The underground church in China is being built on an apostolic foundation. I realized two significant things during our second visit: (1) These brethren are well-equipped in the apostolic grace, and (2) there was an obvious absence of the prophetic grace. Apostles' doctrine was being repeated, but was not being established with the full understanding that comes by grace through prophets. That was our last trip to China. We connected the apostles with prophets who went for some years afterward.

Teachers also fail to understand their role within the context of the whole equipping team ministry. They are to be teaching consistent with, and expanding upon, what the apostles build as foundation, and the prophets establish as foundational understanding.

There is no lack of Westerners who love to learn. Teachers can build significant followings and large ministries based upon their grace to teach. But, apart from apostles and prophets, such efforts fail to bring forth the kingdom *on earth as it is in heaven.*

We also observe that those minds that love to accumulate knowledge are most likely of all people to divide over doctrine. Division itself is the inevitable evidence of carnality, of immaturity.

I could not talk to you as to spiritual [men], but as to nonspiritual [men of the flesh, in whom the carnal nature predominates], as to mere infants [in the new life] in Christ [unable to talk yet!]

I fed you with milk, not solid food, for you were not yet strong enough [to be ready for it]; but even yet you are not strong enough [to be ready for it], for you are still [unspiritual, having the nature] of the flesh [under the control of ordinary impulses]. For as long as [there are] envying and jealousy and wrangling and factions among you, are you not unspiritual and of the flesh, behaving yourselves after a human standard and like mere (unchanged) men?[9]

Surely, *knowledge puffs up.*[10] I have walked with high teaching gifts for years that filter everything I try to say through what they have already determined to be the truth. They are precious in all other respects, embracing love, but lacking in the humility and meekness that could facilitate continuing spiritual growth and development.

Again, let me add this qualification! We have never been exposed to the fullness of equipping graces or the fruit thereof. Consequently, this type of teaching can only be grasped by those who are eagerly seeking first the kingdom of God and His righteousness. Unfortunately, most Christians have found what they were seeking.

IMMATURE AND UNEQUIPPED

The lack of the cohesive and integral graces of *first apostles, second prophets, third teachers*, is evidenced by the exhortation and reproof of the writer of Hebrews:

For though by this time you ought to be teachers, you have need again for someone to teach you the elementary principles of the oracles of God, and you have come to need milk and not solid food. For everyone who partakes only of milk is not accustomed to the word of righteousness, for he is an infant. But solid food is for the mature, who because of practice have their senses trained to discern good and evil.

---

[9] 1 Corinthians 3:1-3 AMPC
[10] 1 Corinthians 8:1

Therefore leaving the elementary teaching about the Christ, let us press on to maturity, not laying again a foundation of repentance from dead works and of faith toward God, of instruction about washings and laying on of hands, and the resurrection of the dead and eternal judgment.[11]

We can conclude from this that the early church itself never came into fruition within its own generation and season. We can know for certain that, from the time of Constantine, the church lost its charismatic nature[12] and became institutionalized. It is our privilege, honor and duty to begin turning the church back to *the simplicity that is in Christ*, and to *the gospel of the kingdom*.

OUR LIFE PARTNER,
THE ABIDING ANOINTING

The gifts that He gives, the grace that He imparts, are resident in Jesus, who is one with the spirits of each member of the new creation. He is our Bridegroom, *Christ in you, the hope of glory.*

*To each one of us grace was given according to the measure of Christ's gift. . . . He who descended is Himself also He who ascended far above all the heavens, **so that He might fill all things**. He gave some as apostles, and some as prophets, and some as evangelists, and some as pastors and teachers.[13]*

Why did Jesus descend from the heavens as an infant, born to a virgin? Why did He grow under the fathering of a carpenter (a builder)? Why did He invest His life in discipling those who would become the apostles of the Lamb? Why did He endure the cross,

---

[11] Hebrews 5:12-14; 6:1-2

[12] The use of "Charismatic nature" is not to be confused with the 20th century charismatic movement. All who are born into the new creation are charismatic because the Spirit of Christ is in them.

[13] Ephesians 4:7; 10-11

demonstrate for all victory over death, and subsequently return to His Father and ours, far above all the heavens? Why?

So that He might fill all things!

Jesus—Apostle, Prophet, Evangelist, Shepherd and Teacher—continues to this day filling people with the Spirit of Himself. Although all of the new creation has the fullness of Jesus abiding within, He severally distributes the manifestations of His Spirit, His gifts, for the common good, to profit withal.

As we see in the example of Zerubbabel, the ones who hold the plumb line in their hands, like master builders or architects, also team with others in the building of the temple, each one according to the grace of God that he/she carries.

Without the coordination of apostles, mutually independent prophets and teachers tend to focus on their favorite topics, leaving the church not established (the prophet role) and not filled (the teacher role).

IT'S TIME TO BUILD THE TEMPLE

When God was speaking in Haggai, he was talking about the rebuilding of the temple:

The word of the Lord came by means of Haggai the prophet [in Jerusalem after the Babylonian captivity] to Zerubbabel son of Shealtiel, governor of Judah, and to Joshua son of Jehozadak, the high priest, saying,

Thus says the Lord of hosts: These people say, The time is not yet come that the Lord's house should be rebuilt [although Cyrus had ordered it done eighteen years before].

Then came the word of the Lord by Haggai the prophet, saying, Is it time for you yourselves to dwell in your paneled houses while this house [of the Lord] lies in ruins?

Now therefore thus says the Lord of hosts: Consider your ways and set your mind on what has come to you. You have sown much, but you have reaped little; you eat, but you do not have enough; you drink, but you do not have your fill; you clothe yourselves, but no one is warm; and he who earns wages has earned them to put them in a bag with holes in it.

Thus says the Lord of hosts: Consider your ways (your previous and present conduct) and how you have fared.[14]

I see the reality of this condition every day as I relate with brethren. They seem so close to breakthrough into the abundant life. Yet, they are not quite where they wish they were, and where God wishes they were. They live in their own houses (ministries), paneled with their own distinctives, rather than building together in the house of the Lord.

Such austerity and frugality does not glorify God. And, I'm not speaking about material luxuries; I'm speaking about kingdom realities . . . *on earth as it is in heaven.*

Now, let's consider some necessary characteristics for those who are sent to build the temple in our midst.

---

[14] Haggai 1:1-7

Chapter 13
ECLECTIC WORKERS NEEDED

It is easy to be dogmatic, to want to push those doctrines that are most important to us. It is not so easy to be eclectic, to "stuff" our "druthers," and find those things that we can agree with when building relationships.

Another descriptive word for our consideration is: *heterogeneous,* meaning consisting of dissimilar or diverse ingredients or constituents. Bingo! This is our 21st century challenge!

We may need a brief refresher regarding the job description of an apostle. In the opening chapter of Part 2 of "The Permanent Revolution" by Alan Hirsch and Tim Catchim, these roles are detailed and explained.

- *Planter*
- *Architect*
- *Foundation layer*
- *Father*
- *Ambassador*

Here is their insightful explanation for *Architect:*

"Our translations use the word 'master builder,' but the exact wording in Greek is *archetekton—arche* meaning origin or first, and *tekton* meaning craftsman or planner, which offers the idea of primary designer or blueprint crafter. The word is loaded with notions of design, innovation, and strategic craftsmanship. Yet unlike modern architects who rarely visit job sites, the cultural understanding of the architect in Paul's day was of one who not only designed the building but directed the building process (1

Corinthians 3:10), Apostolic ministry is on-site work, not just ivory tower ideation."

Apostolic sending is a commission to a work! The Holy Spirit said to the prophets and teachers in Antioch, *"Set apart for Me Barnabas and Saul for **the work** to which I have called them."*[1]

You may remember that Barnabas had gone to find Paul, and brought him to Antioch. We can safely assume that the wisdom Paul carried was significant in laying a foundation in Antioch that the prophets and teachers could build upon.

We may also assume that the Holy Spirit who brought Paul and Barnabas together and used them together in Antioch, then sent them together carrying the credentials proven in Antioch.

Perhaps you will remember Jesus saying, *"The harvest is plentiful, but the laborers (workers) are few; therefore beseech the Lord of the harvest to send out laborers into His harvest.*[2]

This prayer request from Jesus has never been timelier! Much of that harvest is to be found within the various structures of both the traditional and contemporary church systems. A plentiful harvest awaits workers who are eclectic, not dogmatic—"expressing personal opinions or beliefs as if they are certainly correct and cannot be doubted."[3]

None of us, within our own capacities and resources, can be excluded from the human tendency to be dogmatic. It is the grace of God that makes it possible for us to rise up by faith that we don't need to be right to be included in God's service. Dogmatic people are often the way they are because certain beliefs are the foundation of their faith and security. Those who truly know Jesus

---

[1] Acts 13:2
[2] Luke 10:2
[3] Mirriam-Webster.com

are at rest in His assurance. It's not about *what* we know; it's about *Who* we know!

The need for security and/or carnal ambitions is two significant reasons for entering into competition with other congregations or denominations.

Competition sucks, especially where and when it shows up in what is supposed to be the Lord's church. Wherever competition raises its ugly head, we may be right to inquire, "Just whose church are we representing?"

No matter what your field of endeavor—the marketplace, sports, you name it. Competition sucks "self" to the forefront. It sucks the old man of sin back to life. Competition pits ego against ego in every arena, from two little children wanting the same toy, political opponents wanting the same position, to leaders of nations wanting to be top dog.

Elongated seasons of politicking inevitably become contentious. Is there an elephant or a donkey in your room? Or is that Jesus I see on the throne? (Hope so!)

I enjoy watching sports, especially golf, basketball and football. Golf is ladies' and gentlemen's competition. Basketball can be quite physical. But, football . . . I recently watched a team give away an inevitable victory because one member of the team had "issues" and committed three personal fouls in the last two minutes, resulting in the other team being enabled to win by kicking a field goal. Forest Gump wisely and profoundly pronounced: "Stupid is as stupid does."

I understand why people get worked up into a lather over their local or favorite sports team. I wrestle with my old man of flesh whenever watching a sporting event, or political debate, or . . .

We are challenged, being virtually immersed in the world, to not allow the world into our hearts. This challenge includes our work to which we have been sent. We do not have the liberty to take sides in religious debates. We cannot allow the ungodly spirit of competition that is aggressively active in consumer-driven churches to have a place in our thinking.

The same challenge exists where doctrinal dogma has marginalized some congregations and denominations. We can understand the human issues that are rooted in traditions passed from one generation to the next. Most or all of us have likewise been so afflicted and affected by the past. Who wants to admit that their great-grandfather may have been wrong?

We should be intentionally loving (and therefore loveable), respectful and patient as we nurture budding relationships that are essential to our role as 21st century Zerubbabels. Remember our objective: God's kingdom *on earth as it is in heaven*!

We are carrying *the pearl of great price*. We do not want to do or say anything that might hinder our presentation of that *pearl*. For, the obvious beauty and inevitable value of that pearl, when revealed, will cause our precious brethren to be willing to sell everything else and buy the field.

The early church in Jerusalem *continued steadfastly in the apostles' teachings.*[4] The apostles were not burdened in their work by competing doctrinal positions. They were not largely hindered by prophets and teachers who had their own agendas.

When such an agenda or doctrinal issue surfaced, they had the relational infrastructure to rightly respond:

---

[4] Acts 2:42

Some men came down from Judea and began teaching the brethren, "Unless you are circumcised according to the custom of Moses, you cannot be saved." And when Paul and Barnabas had great dissension and debate with them, the brethren determined that Paul and Barnabas and some others of them should go up to Jerusalem to the apostles and elders concerning this issue.[5]

21ˢᵗ century Zerubbabels (apostles) are graced to smooth religious feathers by turning conversations back to the foundation of the church. *For no other foundation can anyone lay than that which is [already] laid, which is Jesus Christ (the Messiah, the Anointed One).*[6]

"When a paradigm shifts, everyone goes back to zero."[7]

When relationships are rightly established and involve trust, because they know that they are loved, they will respond to going back to the cornerstone, Jesus, and begin anew there to plot our course under the shadow of His wings.

The One who teaches us in the moment what to say, or actually speaks through us, knows the needed wisdom to temper us and draw us back into the Spirit realm where security and safety abide.[8]

"My hope is built on nothing less than Jesus' blood and righteousness; I dare not trust the sweetest frame, but wholly lean on Jesus' name. On Christ, the solid Rock, I stand; all other ground is sinking sand."[9]

---

[5] Acts 15:1-2
[6] 1 Corinthians 3:11 AMPC
[7] Joel Barker
[8] Luke 12:12
[9] "My Hope is Built on Nothing Less" by Edward Mote

All apostles are missionaries, but not all missionaries are apostles. All missions are apostolic in nature, but not necessarily led by master builders. Surely, God sends people on missions that are other than being as wise master builders.

There are some who are given to parenting/discipling individuals, thus changing their lives with the hope that they will change their cultures. Some establish institutions, such as orphanages, schools, hospitals, etc., that express the heart of God through educating and healing.

Kerala is the Southwestern-most state in India. While most of India averages fifteen percent of the population Christian, Kerala is forty percent. Even the majority Hindu population acknowledges that Kerala's relatively high ratings in education and medical care are attributed to the contributions made by Christians.

Surely, such work is apostolic by nature, but not necessarily the direct fruit of apostolicity.

Chapter 14

HOLISTIC APOSTOLICITY

*A*nd *He went up on the hillside and called to Him [for Himself] those whom He wanted and chose, and they came to Him. And He appointed twelve to continue to be with Him, and that He might send them out to preach [as apostles or special messengers] and to have authority and power to heal the sick and to drive out demons.*[1]

Luke's account adds a significant element:

Now in those days it occurred that He went up into a mountain to pray, and spent the whole night in prayer to God. And when it was day, He summoned His disciples and selected from them twelve, whom He named apostles (special messengers).[2]

It is easy to conclude that, as Jesus prayed all night, He was going over the list of candidates for apostolicity with the Father. This must be so, for three years later He prayed for them, acknowledging that they were give Him by the Father:

And [now] I am no more in the world, but these are [still] in the world, and I am coming to You. Holy Father, keep in Your Name [in the knowledge of Yourself] those whom You have given Me, that they may be one as We [are one].[3]

Jesus only did what He saw the Father doing.[4] As *the Apostle and High Priest of our confession,*[5] He modeled apostolicity, not only for the apostles who would follow, but also (as we will soon see) for all saints.

---

[1] Mark 3:13-15 AMPC
[2] Luke 6:12-13 AMPC
[3] John 17:11 AMPC
[4] John 5:19-20
[5] Hebrews 3:1

Paul, an apostle—[special messenger appointed and commissioned and sent out] not from [any body of] men nor by or through any man, but by and through Jesus Christ (the Messiah) and God the Father, Who raised Him from among the dead.[6]

VERTICAL & HORIZONTAL RELATIONSHIPS

We know that, sometime later, Paul, along with Barnabas, was *set apart and sent* from the church in Antioch—after fasting and prayer—*"for the work to which I (the Holy Spirit) have called them."[7]*

We can see in the above verses that holistic apostolicity begins with Jesus who calls a man unto Himself, commissions him, and then abides in him to fulfill His purpose through him. The horizontal implications are equally valid and necessary. For no one should be independent and unaccountable. The credibility of the parts of any body is found in interdependence and interaction.

"Apostolic ministry today must have 'relational' authority and accountability with corresponding responsibility! Apostolic ministry is the "delegated authority" commissioned by the Holy Spirit with corresponding responsibility by the authority of the Sender, Jesus Christ Himself!!

"There is a 'mutual accountability' in relational authority that is not based on 'positional authority' but rather based on the responsibility of our love, honor, and respect for each other!!!"[8]

While Scripture clearly acknowledges that apostles are given authority for the building up of the body, it is essential for apostles to be received for that authority to be effective. Our bottom-line

---

[6] Galatians 1:1 AMPC
[7] Acts 13:1-3
[8] Jim Becton

basis for exercising God's authority is rooted in holistic one-anothering:

Look carefully then how you walk! Live purposefully and worthily and accurately, not as the unwise and witless, but as wise (sensible, intelligent people), making the very most of the time [buying up each opportunity], because the days are evil.

Therefore do not be vague and thoughtless and foolish, but understanding and firmly grasping what the will of the Lord is. And do not get drunk with wine, for that is debauchery; but ever be filled and stimulated with the [Holy] Spirit.

Speak out to one another in psalms and hymns and spiritual songs, offering praise with voices [and instruments] and making melody with all your heart to the Lord, at all times and for everything giving thanks in the name of our Lord Jesus Christ to God the Father.

BE SUBJECT TO ONE ANOTHER

Be subject to one another out of reverence for Christ (the Messiah, the Anointed One).[9]

When we receive an apostle in the name of an apostle, we receive an apostle's reward—the equipping apostolic impartation, the grace gift that is sourced in Jesus Christ Himself. Whoever receives an apostle receives Jesus Christ, the Apostle and High Priest of our confession.

"He who receives you receives Me, and he who receives Me receives Him who sent Me."[10]

Heaven's kingdom on earth is nothing like top-down human authority. It is activated by the receiver(s) submission which allows spiritual authority to function. Its purpose and intent is *for building up and not for tearing down* . . . that the brethren may be

---

[9] Ephesians 5:15-21 AMPC
[10] Matthew 10:40

made complete (holistic), be comforted and be like minded, live in peace:

So I write these things while I am absent from you, that when I come to you, I may not have to deal sharply in my use of the authority which the Lord has given me [to be employed, however] for building [you] up and not for tearing [you] down.

Finally, brethren, farewell (rejoice)! Be strengthened (perfected, completed, made what you ought to be); be encouraged and consoled and comforted; be of the same [agreeable] mind one with another; live in peace, and [then] the God of love [Who is the Source of affection, goodwill, love, and benevolence toward men] and the Author and Promoter of peace will be with you.[11]

HOLISTIC APOSTOLICITY IS FOR ALL

Holistic apostolicity is the fruit of the releasing of the other graces to come alongside, and to provide balanced and fully-orbed equipping of the saints for works of service.

Even as some prophets and teachers miss their mark by functioning apart from the grace of apostolicity, some apostles also miss the mark by failing to bring prophets and teachers alongside.

Apostles, particularly those with high teaching gifts, sometimes go beyond the foundation of wise master builders, and try to establish the church in understanding. God intends for this latter work to be accomplished by prophets.

1. Apostles **build the church** with **wisdom**
2. Prophets **establish the church** with **understanding**
3. Teachers **fill the church** with **knowledge**

These apostolic teachers are filling the earth with apologetics for the role of apostle. The actual functioning of apostles should result in the cohesive and integral functions of prophets and teachers.

---

[11] 2 Corinthians 13:10-11 AMPC

In the commissioning of the twelve apostles of the Lamb, Jesus included these words:

*". . . Teaching them to observe **all** that I commanded you . . ."*

This is making reference to what was known by the early church as *the apostles' (foundational) teaching (or doctrine).*[12]

Jesus commanded them to GO, and then immediately commanded them to tell the disciples to GO. Those who are equipped by virtue of the apostolic grace are equipped with apostolicity for their own parts in the missional company. Not all are apostles; all are to be apostolic.

"As you sent Me into the world, I also have sent them into the world."[13]

Then, the heart cry for oneness of all saints was launched toward heaven, from Son to Father:

"Neither for these alone do I pray [it is not for their sake only that I make this request], but also for all those who will ever come to believe in (trust in, cling to, rely on) Me through their word and teaching, that they all may be one, [just] as You, Father, are in Me and I in You, that they also may be one in Us, so that the world may believe and be convinced that You have sent Me.

"I have given to them the glory and honor which You have given Me, that they may be one [even] as We are one: I in them and You in Me, in order that they may become one and perfectly united, that the world may know and [definitely] recognize that You sent Me and that You have loved them [even] as You have loved Me."[14]

---

[12] Acts 2:42
[13] John 17:18
[14] John 17:20-23 AMPC

CHAPTER 15

KINGDOM ECONOMICS 101

It was June 9, 1968, and I, with my family, was sent to the nations by the Holy Spirit, with the laying on of hands by the elders. We left California for New York with our four daughters, a full tank of gas, and eighty-four dollars. We pulled a seventeen-year-old twelve-foot travel trailer rigged to sleep all six of us. Our oldest daughter did the math: "Six people in a twelve-foot trailer. We each get two feet!"

That beat-up and worn-out twelve-foot travel trailer was truly luxurious when compared to the homes of many in Third World nations. I have stepped over sleeping people in airports, train stations, bus depots and on the sidewalks. Some people are born, live and die without ever seeing the inside of a house.

Such experiences serve us well in having a more sensitive and accurate worldview. And only one conclusion comes from such a worldview—an impassioned cry for the kingdom *on earth as it is in heaven!*

I wish that I had and heeded this counsel from Publilius Syrus on the front side of this journey: "If you wish to reach the highest, begin at the lowest."

I thought that I was at the top of my "game" in those early years. Eventually, I came to understand what Paul testified, *"I determined to know nothing among you except Jesus Christ, and Him crucified."*

He went on to say, *"I was with you in weakness and in fear and in much trembling, and my message and my preaching were not in persuasive words of wisdom, but in demonstration of the Spirit and of power, so that your faith would not rest on the wisdom of men, but on the power of God."[1]*

Bottom line, we have been given a stewardship; not ownership!

STEWARDS OF MYSTERIES

"Let a man regard us in this manner, as servants of Christ and stewards of the mysteries of God."[2]

As servants of Christ and stewards of mysteries, we, together, are the temple of the living God; *just as God said, "Therefore, COME OUT FROM THEIR MIDST AND BE SEPARATE," says the Lord. AND DO NOT TOUCH WHAT IS UNCLEAN; And I will welcome you. "And I will be a father to you, and you shall be sons and daughters to Me," says the Lord Almighty.[3]*

A good father disciplines his children, provides their needs, protects them from evil, and guides them into their destiny. Many in this generation are without fathers. But, *we have One in heaven who is our Father.[4] Therefore, we do not lose heart.[5]* We *do not worry about tomorrow.[6]*

Kingdom economics become tangible only as we begin to recognize our *stewardship of the mysteries of God*, and His Fatherly stewardship of us. We begin to grasp the true identity of *the pearl of great price*, and find our hearts willing to sell out in order to clutch that *pearl* close to our heart.

Those of us who eagerly give our entire lives to Jesus—embracing the cross daily in order to be filled with and led by His Spirit—increasingly receive the promised *increase* that He gives.

---

[1] 1 Corinthians 2:2-5
[2] 1 Corinthians 4:1
[3] 2 Corinthians 6:17-18
[4] Matthew 23:9
[5] 2 Corinthians 4:16
[6] Matthew 6:34

RESOLUTE AND CONSECRATED

"No one can serve two masters; for either he will hate the one and love the other, or he will stand by and be devoted to the one and despise and be against the other. You cannot serve God and mammon (deceitful riches, money, possessions, or whatever is trusted in)."[7]

Our understanding of *mammon* has been greatly enlarged as our hearts have been gradually prepared to release what we had previously *worshiped*. (We didn't know how comprehensive *worship* can be.) The stripping actually comes into focus only after we have laid our eyes upon the pearl, and we are awaiting our new levels of faith and commitment.

All along, we had thought that we were totally committed, without reservation. Yes, we had sold the field to Jesus in a critically decisive moment. However, the mining of the field for the royal treasure takes a lifetime. That's how we go from glory to glory. That's how we grow from faith to faith. And that's how we increase from strength to strength. Yes, that's how we grow.

Our potential is already in our possession. But, our discovery comes gradually as the Spirit of God within patiently and lovingly clears away the rubble of our self-limiting humanity, and unearths the eternal riches of His glory within these earthen vessels.

Stewarding by the hand of God has kept intact all that He placed in us while we were yet in our mothers' wombs. He waited for us during all of those moments, hours, days, months and years when we were busy stewarding our own *rubbish* as though it was of some significance and value.

---

[7] Matthew 6:24 AMPC

WAITING UPON HIM WHO WAITS FOR US

We, too, have taken our journeys on the road to Damascus, not having any idea of what (or Who) awaits around the next bend to invade us, intervene at just the right moment, and replace our lives forever with His own.[8] We, too, can identify with Paul's testimony to that life-changing encounter.

We would do well to slowly and prayerfully consider these four verses in the Amplified Bible, Classic Edition:

Whatever former things I had that might have been gains to me, I have come to consider as [one combined] loss for Christ's sake. Yes, furthermore, I count everything as loss compared to the possession of the priceless privilege (the overwhelming preciousness, the surpassing worth, and supreme advantage) of knowing Christ Jesus my Lord and of progressively becoming more deeply and intimately acquainted with Him [of perceiving and recognizing and understanding Him more fully and clearly]. For His sake I have lost everything and consider it all to be mere rubbish (refuse, dregs), in order that I may win (gain) Christ (the Anointed One),

And that I may [actually] be found and known as in Him, not having any [self-achieved] righteousness that can be called my own, based on my obedience to the Law's demands (ritualistic uprightness and supposed right standing with God thus acquired), but possessing that [genuine righteousness] which comes through faith in Christ (the Anointed One), the [truly] right standing with God, which comes from God by [saving] faith.

[For my determined purpose is] that I may know Him [that I may progressively become more deeply and intimately acquainted with Him, perceiving and recognizing and understanding the wonders of His Person more strongly and more clearly], and that I may in

---

[8] Galatians 2:20

that same way come to know the power outflowing from His resurrection [which it exerts over believers], and that I may so share His sufferings as to be continually transformed [in spirit into His likeness even] to His death, [in the hope that if possible I may attain to the [spiritual and moral] resurrection [that lifts me] out from among the dead [even while in the body].[9]

So, 21st century Zerubbabels, those with the passion of Paul, *whose strength is in God, in whose hearts are the highways of Zion*, hear the word of the Lord:

"Do not store up for yourselves treasures on earth, where moth and rust destroy, and where thieves break in and steal. But store up for yourselves treasures in heaven, where neither moth nor rust destroys, and where thieves do not break in or steal; for where your treasure is, there your heart will be also.

GOD'S TREASURES ARE PEOPLE

God treasures people. He began His earth adventure by creating an eco-balanced environment conducive for life of all kinds. We might call it "a garden." He then created us, male and female, and gave us dominion over all creation, placing us in the garden to manage and tend it.

We are the pinnacle of all creation, created in God's image and likeness, to do just as we see our Father doing. His ultimate intention is to fill the earth with His glory. Only people created in God's image can carry His glory.

God spoke to the fathers in the prophets about the provision for our sonship and the consummation of the glory of His kingdom—*on earth, as it is in heaven.*

He made known to us the mystery of His will, according to His kind intention which He purposed in Him with a view to an administration suitable to the fullness of times, that is, the summing up of all things in Christ, things in the heavens and things on the earth.

---

[9] Philippians 3:7-11 AMPC

At the appointed moment that I exit this dimension to take my place among the cloud of witnesses, I will leave empty-handed. My storehouse is filled with people. They are His treasure and mine. They are my first stewarding responsibility.

This is only one aspect of the multidimensional storehouse of heaven. It is undoubtedly first of the Master's checklist.

"For God so greatly loved and dearly prized the world that He [even] gave up His only begotten (unique) Son, so that whoever believes in (trusts in, clings to, relies on) Him shall not perish (come to destruction, be lost) but have eternal (everlasting) life.

"For God did not send the Son into the world in order to judge (to reject, to condemn, to pass sentence on) the world, but that the world might find salvation and be made safe and sound through Him."[10]

Only when people have first place in our ministerial agenda will we be rightly ready to represent the King and His glorious kingdom. As His love "leaks" through our brokenness, others will know that we care.

Zerubbabel's storehouse for his temple-building project was lined with wood from the mountain. Ours are those who are being quarried so that they may be built together into God's house, made without hands, with living stones.

"Fear of differences is fear of life itself. It is possible to conceive of conflict as not necessarily a wasteful outbreak of incompatibilities but a normal process by which socially valuable differences register themselves for the enrichment of all."[11]

"If *glory* is a manifestation of God's unique 'godlikeness,' then *honor* is the correct recognition of that glory in another."[12] Only as we walk together in faith, truly honoring one another in love, will we manifest the kingdom for others to see.

---

[10] John 3:16-17 AMPC
[11] Mary Parker Follett
[12] Paul Manwaring

Chapter 16

KICK THE CAN OR CHANGE COURSE

At the time of this writing, the United States of America is reaping the harvest of irresponsible and undisciplined fiscal policies that literally threaten its future. Many politicians prefer to kick the can (the responsibility of facing issues and making changes) down the road to our children and grandchildren, rather than making the hard choices today. Making such choices could negatively affect their electability, because their constituencies are overbalanced by the numbers of those demanding and cleaving to what they call *entitlements*.

Irresponsibility overshadows a vast contingent of the voting block. If they only knew what we are really entitled to, they would cry out for mercy!

I believe better of us! I believe that we are, for the most part, unaware of the tragic kicking of the can of spiritual responsibility for nearly two thousand years. The fiscal condition of the USA should not become a parable or metaphor of the church of the 21st century.

Perhaps you have read this far, an indication that you really care. Your very livelihood is wrapped in leading a network of individual congregations spread across many states, or even nations.

Perhaps you are fathering an apostolic center, a model congregation where other church leaders come for envisioning and instruction. Perhaps you are preparing young adults and sending them back into their own home towns.

Maybe you are the founder and leader of a mega-church where thousands are being nurtured through the grace that is on your life.

Your various campuses are influencing many regions in your city. And your local and regional benevolence contributions and efforts are truly impacting many.

Or, you have developed a parachurch ministry that focuses upon a singular purpose that the church has been neglecting. You are really doing the work of the church, but not within a particular denominational or congregational setting.

I personally know some wonderful brothers who are graced for apostolicity, and have done what they know to do. Most of them fit in one or more of the above categories. Realizing what a dramatic challenge this book is to some of them requires some explanation based upon the fact of my love for and belief in them.

I remember Jesus' words regarding those who loved the approval of men, and were not willing to risk being put out of the synagogue:

Jesus cried aloud, "Every man who believes in Me, is believing in the One who sent Me; and every man who sees Me is seeing the One who sent Me. I have come into the world as light, so that no one who believes in Me need remain in the dark. Yet, if anyone hears My sayings and does not keep them, I do not judge him—for I did not come to judge the world but to save it. Every man who rejects Me and will not accept My sayings has a judge—at the last day, the very words that I have spoken will be his judge."[1]

We do not need to repeat history again and again. We are all brothers. And we can be convicted by the Holy Spirit speaking through one another. We can be assured that God has just the right strategy for each one of us to make corrections and adjustments accordingly. We can also call upon and sit in counsel with one another as we take up the challenge for 21st century Zerubbabels.

---

[1] John 12:44-48 J. B. Phillips

Today, in most cities and regions, there are groups of living stones gathering together in various locations and venues, with various flavors of emphasis—various distinctives that divide.

Even those of us who consider ourselves to be apostolic have done the same thing. It would appear that we are hopelessly divided. And, it is understandable for us to not want to rock the boat in which our financial stability is floating.

So, do we faithfully and obediently change course as the Spirit leads us? Or, do we kick the can down the road to yet another generation, leaving them with the same marred and scarred history that we inherited from our forefathers?

21st century Zerubbabels have responded to the missional passion of Jesus in many venues. As He said, *"The harvest is plentiful, but the laborers are few."* [2] Every generation must retrofit its missional strategy, making adjustments to fit the prevailing cultures where we live and serve.

Is there a generation of Jesus people in the earth today who will not simply change the venue and the program, but will make the radical adjustments needed to return to an understanding that the church is one?

Is there a generation of Jesus people who are willing to be radicalized to recognize one another after the Spirit and— in faith and humility—*be subject to one another in the fear of Christ?* [3]

"When the forms of an old culture are dying, the new culture is created by a few people who are not afraid to be insecure."
- Rudolph Bahro

"To encounter God is to change." – Dietrich Bonhoeffer

---

[2] Luke 10:2
[3] Ephesians 5:21

"Do the best you can until you know better. Then, when you know better, do better." – Maya Angelou

Appendix 1
LEADER-SHIFT
David Orton

If David is the proto-typical man of God's government, Saul is the proto-typical man of human government.

Just as Israel opted for Saul, rejecting Samuel the man of the Spirit, the church likewise rejected their men of the Spirit, the apostles and prophets. They opted instead for the `monarchical bishop', in effect, like Israel, they had said, "Give us a king to be like all the other nations!" (1 Sam 8:5). Human government kicked in, setting the pattern for hierarchical leadership mentalities and structures to this day.

However, in obscurity God prepared a man, David, who in the fullness of time would receive the kingdom. Likewise today, the kingdom is being taken from Saul-leaders and given to a Davidic company prepared of God. There is a shift right now from human to divine leadership. And just as David submitted to wilderness preparations, experiencing many perplexing dealings, so too this emerging company. Their hearts of pride and self-sufficiency have been humbled through life's experiences and they are currently sensing the stirrings of imminent destiny fulfillment, inquiring of the Lord, "Is this the time to go up..." (1 Sam 2:1). Timing is everything right now (I will comment more on this in Part 3).

David was a `processed' man. He had been through the deep heart searchings and brokenness necessary for leadership in the kingdom. In the fullness of time God drew him out of the "valley of the shadow of death" raising him to the throne. Tragically this is not often the case with today's leaders and was not so with Saul.

While Saul was not a `processed' man he was "head and shoulders" above his peers (1 Sam 9:2). He stood out from among the crowd as a man with all the natural attributes of leadership. Saul-leadership is characterized by the "head" and by the "shoulders"— by human thinking and strength. In man's estimation he was an obvious choice. In fact, he was effectively the people's choice (see 1 Sam 8:5 ff). Contemporary leadership culture in the church focuses either more on the "head" through education and natural thinking or on the "shoulders" through management and people skills than on a heart processed by God. Intimacy with God and acquaintance with his dealings, let alone a sovereign supernatural call and preparation, overall are not prerequisites for today's ministry.

David on the other hand was not the obvious choice. The youngest son of Jesse he was forgotten and clearly not considered a front-runner when Samuel visited looking to anoint the new king (see 1 Sam 16). After viewing all the obvious choices the Lord reminded Samuel,

Samuel, don't think Eliab is the one just because he's tall and handsome. He isn't the one I've chosen. People judge others by what they look like, but I judge people by what is in their hearts. 1Sa 16:7 CEV

God's choice is not based on human considerations. Who we may think is a natural and obvious leader is not often the one God chooses. He sees through the talent and natural attributes to the heart. This is where the issues of life are decided (see Prov 4:23). And it is where the *leader-shift* in the church is occurring right now. Many in the past season have been making decisions at a heart level which will now play out at ground level. The things that have been hidden will now be made visible.

A judgment is about to be pronounced over the old order:

But now your kingdom shall not endure. The Lord has sought out for Himself a man after His own heart, and the Lord has appointed him as ruler over His people, because you have not kept what the Lord commanded you. 1Sa 13:14 NASB"

Excerpt from *"The Saul-David Transition - Part 2"*

www.lifemessenger.org

APOSTOLIC CHARACTER

Art Katz
(February 13, 1929 – June 28, 2007)

(This is Chapter 6 - From the book *"Apostolic Foundations"* by Art Katz. It was my privilege to meet Art on several occasions in the 1970s and 1980s when we were both parts of a fellowship of apostles and prophets that met together twice each year. I contend that a primary role of New Covenant prophets is to establish the church in understanding the apostolic role and foundation. Here is a clear example of that priority. – Don Atkin)

Apostolic meekness[1] is that quality of character by which we shall be able to discern those who "say they are apostles and are not." Presumptuous apostles are going to be one of the dangers in the Last Days. They will seem to have a measure of authority and knowledge that will impress the undiscerning. There is, however, one measure of authenticity that cannot be feigned or emulated, namely, true meekness. Meekness is not something one learns at school, but something attained by men and women under the hand of God, in union with Him. He is meekness. In other words, it can only be given out of a man's proximity with God, who Himself is meek and lowly of heart; there is no other way to obtain it.

Moses, who wrote the first five books of the Bible, could say of himself, "Moses was the meekest man on the face of the earth." It sounds like arrogance of spirit, but when a man can speak that of himself, knowing he cannot take to himself any acknowledgment for that condition, then we have an ultimate humility. God's grace had brought him to that meekness. Humility is not something that

---

[1] "Apostolic meekness should be the character of the entire body of Christ, the fruit of apostolic equipping by example and impartation." – Don Atkin

man can work up by himself on the earth, and develop as a character trait. Humility is what God is in Himself, and the only one who will display and exhibit it, is that one who has been consistently in the presence of God's humility. It is humbling to be there, and that is why Moses could make that statement, not as a credit to himself, but to God, out of whose presence that humility was established.

The call to communion with God is never going to be convenient. There is a dying in order to find one's way into the place of the secret council of God, and one cannot enter it with the spirit of expediency. Expediency is contrary to God's Spirit and wisdom. God's call to Moses was to come up unto Him. It was not for any benefit Moses was going to receive—even spiritual benefit, but rather a seeking of God for His own sake, and without any regard to the benefit accruing to the seeker by so doing.

It is interesting to note Moses' disposition on coming down from the Mount with the tablets of the Law. When he saw Israel dancing round the golden calf, he burned with indignation and anger, and threw down the tablets of the Law that were written by the finger of God Himself. He then commanded that the golden calf be granulated and ground to powder, and that the people Israel were to drink it. He made them drink their idol, and you do not hear a single complaint or whimper of opposition to that requirement. Evidently, he came with such an authority that no one in any way took issue with that stipulation.

There is a conjunction between humility and authority. The first expression of Moses' humility was an expression of authority of such a magnitude that no one questioned it. Then he asked who was going to be on the Lord's side, and the Levites came forward. They were told to put their swords on their side, and go into the camp, slaying all those who had gone whoring after false gods, including friends and relatives. What authority for the man who was the meekest in all the earth! It is only because he was the meekest that the authority was his, and the densest of souls recognized it. They could not, therefore, offer up a quibble of opposition. He was 'very God' in his indignation and authority, and his meekness was the statement, not of some affectation or superficial polish, but of a union with God in such a way, that God's very own character was imparted to him.

The Apostle Paul himself was unsparing in telling things the way they needed to be spoken. He rebuked, exhorted, beseeched and pleaded. However, he did not flaunt his apostolic credentials, nor did he employ his authority to coerce and manipulate. He entreated, *"I entreat you as a father ... I beseech you, by the mercies of God, that you present ...."* This is a distinctive character of the apostolic mindset and character. It does not employ its authority in any coercive way. The use of authority reveals us, and someone has said, "What we do with the weakest and the least is what we are." When a nation begins to oppress and persecute the weak and defenseless, it is revealing its true and ugly character.

HUMILITY IS OBEDIENCE

The issue of humility is paradoxical, because the apostle is so single eyed, adamant, and utterly persuaded about the rightness of his word, that it appears as arrogance. I suspect that the false apostle is self-defacing. He will appear humble, something like a 'salesman's humility' that is put into effect in order to sell the product. If we are going to be a discerning church, which is to say, an apostolic church, then the issue of authentic humility needs to come into our consciousness. The quality of true meekness, which Paul had, despite his uncompromising references to himself, seems to be arrogant, and yet right there, is the true meekness.

The Lord Himself was absolute, using language in such a fierce way. He acted in a way that seems to suggest anything but humility. For example, in overthrowing the moneychanger's tables, it would appear that, for that moment at least, He laid aside His meekness, and was acting now in another character. Was He meek even while He was violent and offensive? This act set in motion the things that eventuated in His death. So how do we reconcile the act of violence that Jesus performed as opposed to what we know of the meekness of God? When we think of meek, we think of mild, quiet and deferring. This is an aggressive and violent act, and yet we are saying that it is meek.

If we see meekness as total obedience to God, and even more in an act, or a word, that would give an impression to the contrary, we will have a greater understanding of its reality. It may even make the obedient servant open to reproach for being violent, or being too zealous, or whatever it is. In other words, Jesus overthrew the moneychangers' tables as an act of humility, because He was submitted to the will of the Father to obey in the moment that it was required, even though it was contrary to His own disposition or personality. He was a meek man, obeying the will of the Father, whose moment of judgment for that Temple had come, and it was performed with a total passion in His jealousy for the glory of God. True humility is reflected in true obedience.

There are instances where God will call us to obedience that seem to contradict meekness, and it would be arrogant not to obey, even by employing the excuse, "It is not my personality. It is not the way that I like to be, because I want the favor and the approval of men to see me as a nice guy, and therefore, I want always to be reasonable, quiet and diplomatic." Yes, you will be applauded for that, but not in heaven. In heaven, it is clear rebellion, because if God wanted you to be 'violent,' and you withheld because it contradicts your personality, or anything like that, you are putting something above and before God, namely, your own self-consideration.

A true apostle will not relent or refrain when God requires him to speak. He shuns the distinctions and honors that men accord each other. He necessarily has to, or there would be a compromising of what he is in God. He is scrupulous in character, and will never use his position to obtain personal advantage. He is naturally unaffected, normal and unprepossessing in appearance and demeanor, despising what is showy, sensational or bizarre. He will not call any attention to himself by external attire. He is the thing in himself, in the very marrow of his being, because of his communion with God, and his history in God. Meekness is the characteristic sign of the authentic apostle, and the quintessential character of God. Based on this, a false apostle, or a false bearer of God's word, can be identified as one who gives the impression of being self-sufficient, always in his dignity, or he affects something to make sure that you have noticed him for his distinctiveness.

UNSELFCONSCIOUS HUMILITY

"The true character of the loveliness that tells for God is always unconscious," wrote Oswald Chambers.

Self-conscious spirituality is where you examine yourself for an ostensibly good thing, even of a spiritual kind, but the very fact that you examine yourself ruins it. True spirituality is unselfconscious; it is mindless about itself. It is the very quality exhibited by Jesus, and though He knew who He was, and disputed with the doctors of the Law at the age of twelve, His whole earthly ministry had a remarkable quality of unselfconsciousness about it. He is not a man who went around making known to what ministry He was called. It is just a wonderful mindlessness, not in the sense of being irresponsible, but where you are not exalted in your own calling. If we say, "Oh, I wonder, do you think God could use me? I wonder if I am of any use." Though it may sound modest and self-effacing in our ears, it is yet corruption. It still has our "I" at the center, and it is that very thing which taints the spiritual life. We need to come into that wonderful place of complete unselfconsciousness, where we are what we are by the grace of God. We do not ever think in terms of ourselves. We simply are, and in that condition, we are a blessing to God and others.

THE BROKEN ALABASTER VIAL

There is an episode in the life of Jesus, hardly worth mentioning, you would think, and yet God includes it in three of the gospels in one form or the other.

And while He was in Bethany at the home of Simon the leper, and reclining at the table, there came a woman with an alabaster vial and poured it over His head. But some were indignantly remarking to one another, "Why has this perfume been wasted? For this perfume might have been sold for over three hundred denarii, and the money given to the poor." And they were scolding her.

But Jesus said, "Let her alone; why do you bother her? She has done a good deed to Me. For the poor you always have with you, and whenever you wish, you can do them good; but you do not always have Me. She has done what she could; she has anointed My body beforehand for the burial. And truly I say to you, wherever the gospel is preached in the whole world, that also which this woman has done shall be spoken of in memory of her."

And Judas Iscariot, who was one of the twelve, went off to the chief priests, in order to betray Him to them. And they were glad when they heard this, and promised to give him money. And he began seeking how to betray Him at an opportune time.[2]

It is not a coincidence that there is a conjunction between this lavish outpouring, and the response to the Lord by Judas and the chief priests, whose betrayal was for the sake of convenience. Jesus said that what she had done would be spoken of in memory of her. That is rather exuberant praise and acknowledgment for

---

[2] Mark 14:3-11

what seems to men, and even to the disciples of Jesus a waste. Efficiency and utility are the spirit of our age, and says, if you invest, or give of something, you expect a payoff and recompense. But something that is given lavishly, without any thought of return, is costly. It made even the disciples to recoil in indignation and to murmur against this woman, and to say, "For what purpose was this waste. That expensive ointment could have been sold and the proceeds used to buy tracts and finance ministries, and done all those wonderfully helpful things." We need to dissuade believers away from the preeminent fascination for ministry. We are so ministerial-minded, and we want so to come into our ministries, and a lot of souls are made shipwreck by a premature coming into ministry when there had been no attention to the foundation of relationship with God and men.

This woman came bearing an extraordinarily exquisite, alabaster vial. The remarkable thing is that there is no way to extract the ointment unless the container is broken. There was no screw-off cap that could be neatly screwed back on for the next time. It was either to break it in order to extract the contents, or the contents remained enclosed. That is a beautiful picture of ourselves, shaped at the hand of God, vials of expensive material, but however outwardly impressive we are in that sense, it will not make us significant to a dying world, and especially to a Jewish people. The thing that makes us significant is rather the fragrance of the knowledge of Him made manifest by us in every place.

We all emit a particular fragrance. With some, the aroma is exquisite, but with others, it is rather ordinary. It depends very much upon what kind of history we have with God, and how deep we are identified with Him in His sufferings, His misunderstandings, His rejections, and all of the things that inhere in a true faith and a true walk. It is one thing to have that fragrance of Christ formed in us through identification with Him, and quite another to have the religion of convenience, which is also the religion of betrayal. If our Christianity costs nothing, and is convenient, we are already one with Judas. The faith is extraordinarily demanding, and that is why Jesus commended what the woman had done, and it was to be a memorial to her wherever this gospel is preached. The gospel is the gospel of extravagant abandonment and pouring out, or it is not the gospel.

Watchman Nee has said that the principle of waste is the principle of power, and we are powerless because we have played it 'close to the vest.' We have not given of ourselves the time, the patience, the misunderstanding, and the vulnerability of pouring ourselves out to each other that would make church the church. We are robbed, therefore, of the potential to form an apostolic body where men can be sent who can preach. We have opted for a religion of convenience, namely, no fuss, no stoop and no bother. That is why Jesus loved this woman, *"She has done a good deed to Me."* If there is any odious phrase to God, it is a work that man performs. He has no respect for the works of men, but He called what this woman did a good deed or work. She came with something very precious and expensive, and she came into a room full of men bristling with indignation, but she did not let that deter her. Moreover, wherever extravagance for Christ's sake is poured out, there will be a corresponding opposition.

There is something lacking in today's church, namely, a pouring out that releases the flow of His Life to the unbelieving world. We are antiseptic and correct, but we are not fragrant. We are not lavish with each other, afraid to take the risks of that kind of intensity of relationship by which alone true apostolic formation of character takes place. We are satisfied with a religion of convenience—a Sunday service and midweek Bible study, and then retreat again to our own privacy.

There is something about brokenness in God's sight that is so dear to Him. It was also exemplified in His own body at the Cross, and He is waiting for the same thing in His church, namely, a broken and contrite people who exude the fragrance of Christ. Something more than correctness and well-meaning intention is required. The meekness of brokenness comes when we come, break, and pour. Meekness is the apostolic distinctive, the fragrance of the knowledge of Him, and every true work is an exercise in humiliation, suffering and death, and emits, therefore, the fragrance of God.

MEEKNESS—THE KEY TO REVELATION

The church is built on the foundation of the apostles and prophets, and a distinction of what is apostolic is the stewardship of the mysteries. The church itself should have this same disposition toward mystery, and the things that can only be revealed. The key to apostolic or prophetic seeing, and the receiving of the revelation of the mysteries of God is found in Ephesians 3:8,

> *"To me, the very least of all saints, this grace was given, to preach to the Gentiles the unfathomable riches of Christ."*

In other words, all true seeing is given to men like Paul, who see themselves as the 'very least of all saints.' Paul is not being deferential or polite. He actually saw himself as this. He was the apostle to whom was afforded such magnitude of visions that God had to give him a thorn in his side, lest he be exalted beyond measure for the revelations that were given him. We must not, therefore, pass by apostolic character, which is to say, the deep humility, the authentic meekness and the Christ-likeness of the apostolic man.

We know that one of the deceptions of the Last Days is false apostles and false prophets. Even now, it is becoming popular where everybody seems to be a prophet today, or even an apostle. They are also quite clever as they have studied and know how to appropriate Paul's counsel and advice, and know when to apply it, and mediate over church issues, etc. Is that, however, the foundational man upon whom the church is built? If the man is the thing in himself, then it is more than his knowledge of church administration, or founding a fellowship. It is his very life; it is his character; it is his knowledge of God. It is what he communicates as one who comes to us out of God's own presence. This statement, 'the very least of all saints' is not Paul being self-deferring, but Paul's actual, stricken, heartfelt consciousness of how he sees himself before God.

It is a remarkable irony that the deeper we grow in the knowledge of God, the more we see ourselves as less. Instead of becoming more exalted by the increase of our knowledge of God, we see how abased and pitiful we really are. It is a contradiction and a paradox, only to be found in God's church. Authentic meekness or humility is not something that one can learn, pick up at school, or take to oneself, but the work of God out of a relationship with Him. It is the revelation of God as He is, and the depths of God, that bring a man to this kind of awareness of his own self. The revelation of what we are is altogether related to the revelation of who God is. The two things always go together.

> *"Then I (Isaiah) said, 'Woe is me, for I am ruined! Because I am a man of unclean lips, and I live among a people of unclean lips; for my eyes have seen the King, the Lord of hosts.'"[3]*

This is the prince of prophets, Isaiah, speaking here. The foundation of the church is the revelation of God as He in fact is. That is the foundation. It is not as we think Him to be, which is more often than not a projection of the way we would like Him to be, especially when we have chosen to celebrate one attribute of God, and ignore another. The key knowledge is the knowledge of God as He is, and the foundational men to the church are those who can communicate God in that knowledge. Paul had this knowledge because he saw himself as the "least of all saints."

---

[3] Isaiah 6:5

THE TWO WITNESSES

"And I will grant authority to my two witnesses, and they will prophesy for twelve hundred and sixty days, clothed in sackcloth. These are the two olive trees and the two lamp-stands that stand before the Lord of the earth.

And if anyone desires to harm them, fire proceeds out of their mouth and devours their enemies; and if anyone would desire to harm them, in this manner he must be killed.

These have the power to shut up the sky, in order that rain may not fall during the days of their prophesying; and they have power over the waters to turn them into blood, and to smite the earth with every plague, as often as they desire."[4]

These men will be dressed in sackcloth, clothed in humility, clothed in the meekness of God. Meekness, as we have said, cannot be learned. Any humility that is obtained through self-conscious determination is necessarily false. The humility of God is a prerequisite for the anointing oil of God, being able to 'shut up the sky' at our will, as we see fit. God can only commit such remarkable dimensions to those who are in authentic union with Him, and the evidence of which is their meekness and humility. The sackcloth is not an external thing, although I am sure it will be worn; it was rather a statement of an inward condition that cannot be effected, and cannot be a technique that we can learn by modulating our voices, or being self-effacing and self-deferring. Either it is, or it is not, and it if is, it will be in proportion to our union with God in the fellowship of His sufferings.

This is how we obtain and maintain a condition of humility, which is the sine qua non, that which is absolutely and essentially

---

[4] Revelation 11:3-6

necessary for the overcoming and authentically spiritual life. This is critical, because we are in a special place of jeopardy. I say 'we' especially to those of us who have a consciousness of being part of the remnant people of God. The very awareness that we are a remnant is the very same thing that can cultivate a place of pride and exclusivity.

Jesus knew He was the Son of God, and that He was sent of the Father, and yet He walked through His life in such a selflessness and mindlessness about His own calling. Paul was like that too, and could say, "Imitate me as I imitate Christ. Follow me in all my ways, and if you do not, you are likely out of the faith," and yet there is no arrogance. It is an ultimate union with God, and it is something we need to be jealous for, or we will find ourselves entrapped and ensnared, not by our defects, but by our virtues. Our virtues can, in this sense, lead us into destruction, more so than our defects.

The gospel is always a call to humility. There is a deep pharisaic root in man that wants to predicate the privileges of God based on merit or works. God goes out of His way to choose the foolish, the weak, and beggarly thing, in fact all that is opposed and contrary to what man would have chosen. Part of our problem is that we do not understand how much God abhors what is in man. He simply would not entrust Himself to man, for He knew what was in man.

BLAMELESS CONSISTENCY

"For our gospel did not come to you in word only, but also in power and in the Holy Spirit and with full conviction; just as you know what kind of men we proved to be among you for your sake."[5]

---

[5] 1 Thessalonians 1:5

There is a theme struck in that one verse, which needs to penetrate our deepest consciousness. Our modern life tends to be set in compartments: the secular, the sacred, everyday life, and the religious, the private person and the public minister, and yet Paul did not know those distinctions. He was one true man through and through, the full-orbed man. The apostle is the thing in himself, the Word made flesh, and that is why Paul could continually offer himself as an example. He did not say, "Follow my principles!" but *"Follow me!"* God does not say that it is the principles of the apostles and prophets that are the foundation of the church, but rather the men in themselves, and what they are in themselves in Christ. We are to be one true thing throughout, day in and day out. Paul was instant in season and out, always ready, always appropriate, before Jews and before Greeks. God's call is for an entire church to be like that.

Paul says,

> *"For our gospel did not come to you in word only, but also in power and in the Holy Spirit and with full conviction; just as you know what kind of men we proved to be among you for your sake."*[6]

There is an equation here: The power of the gospel in full conviction was in exact proportion to the quality, character and manner of men they proved to be among them. The authority and power that Paul exhibited was altogether in proportion to the kind of man he proved to be, and he says this to the church that was saved by his own witness.

There are false apostles everywhere, and you can identify them because they let you know they are apostles. They have flair and a facility, they can quote Scripture, they can interpolate and quote Pauline things, and one could almost be impressed. They have such

---

[6] 1 Thessalonians 1:5

a manner, but it was not Paul's way. Paul could say to the Thessalonians, *"just as you know what kind of men we proved to be among you for your sake."* In other words, in all seasons, they knew Paul as the same, consistent thing, and this was altogether related to the word that came to them in power. There was no professional ministerial mystique in Paul by which he was something else privately.

There are only two ruling passions in an apostolic man, namely, *"for your sake and for God's sake."* It was never for our sake. Paul had no interest in himself, or for himself. These two considerations are the necessary requirements for an apostle, and therefore an apostolic church. The superstructure must be of the same kind as the foundation. In his farewell address to the elders in Ephesus, Paul said,

> *"You yourselves know, from the first day that I set foot in Asia, how I was with you the whole time, serving the Lord with all humility and with tears and with trials which came upon me through the plots of the Jews;"*[7]

Regardless of his outward circumstances, there was a precious consistency of character. There is no place here for human moodiness, or a complaining spirit. This is something far beyond human good intention, and there is only one way to explain this kind of consistency, as in Paul's own words: *"For to me, to live is Christ."* This is not a fanciful expression, a kind of apostolic extravagance, but Paul being quite literal. This is the only answer, and everything else is an invitation to catastrophe. We cannot seek to be apostolic, or true, based on human determination by which we bite our lips, not knowing what we ought to be doing. We will fail, and we will fail wretchedly. We must find the mystery that Paul found, and it is just as available to us as it was to him, but we

---

[7] Acts 20:18b-19

have not believed the Word, and we have not wanted to receive its meaning.

There is only one explanation for the phenomenon of Paul. His life was the very continuation of the crucified and resurrected Christ, who had found for Himself another body wholly yielded to His life. It was a Paul who had no life unto himself, or for himself, and who could say, *"I am crucified with Christ, nevertheless I live, yet not I."* Do you know why we have not stumbled on this stupefying requirement? It is because we have been content to live beneath the apostolic level. We have not felt this kind of requirement of character to be incumbent for us, and therefore we have been satisfied to be 'nice guys,' or our standard is a standard of 'Christian respectability,' and of being pleasant and polite. But I want to ask you a question: Is our gospel going forth in the power of the Spirit, and in full conviction? Paul says to these Thessalonians,

> *"For they themselves report about us what kind of a reception we had with you, and how you turned to God from idols to serve a living and true God, and to wait for His Son from heaven, whom He raised from the dead, that is Jesus, who delivers us from the wrath to come."* [8]

For all of our modern day, innocuous evangelism, flashy evangelists, and 'decisions for Christ' that are made, can it be said in today's proclamation of the gospel that pagans are turned from idols to serve the true and living God?

The power, however, in Paul's gospel and the conviction of it was sufficient to turn pagans from their idols to serve a living God. How many of us even have this as the criterion in our evangelistic work? Our standards have fallen wretchedly! We are content if men will only 'accept' Christ, and continue to attend Christian

---

[8] 1 Thessalonians 1:9-10

services, but no great requirement is made of them. Our evangelism has become a kind of 'statistical' game. How many have made decisions, and yet remain essentially 'pagans'? However, Paul's gospel had another consequence; it turned men from their idols to serve the living God, which is more than merely attending services. Our whole standard needs to be elevated again to the apostolic level, for this alone is God's. In addition, I want to reiterate my point: it will never be so, and our gospel will not have full conviction and power until we come to the place of apostolic selflessness, where we are wholly abandoned to the purposes of God. We are mindless about our security, our condition, and our pleasure. One can abound, or one can abate; it does not matter. Paul says in Acts 20:22–24a:

"And now, behold, bound in the spirit, I am on my way to Jerusalem, not knowing what will happen to me there, except that the Holy Spirit solemnly testifies to me in every city, saying that bonds and afflictions await me. But I do not consider my life of any account as dear to myself..."

Here we see the divine character wrought in a man, who was originally a persecutor and a murderer. It is going to require all of eternity to reveal the kindness of His grace toward us, not only in this age, but also in the ages to come. Paul did not consider his life of any account as dear to himself, and we shall never have the power and authority to turn men from their idols so long as we hold our lives as dear to ourselves. Paul was impervious to things, and we need to come into that apostolic condition. In 1 Corinthians 7:29–32a Paul states:

"But this I say, brethren, the time has been shortened, so that from now on those who have wives should be as though they had none; and those who weep, as though they did not weep; and those who rejoice, as though they did not rejoice; and those who buy, as though they did not possess; and those who use the world, as though they did not make

154

full use of it; for the form of this world is passing away. But I want you to be free from concern ..."

The whole purpose of this apostolic exhortation is that we may attend upon the Lord without distraction, for the time is short! He said that almost two thousand years ago, but how many of us believe it now? They lived in the expectation of an apocalyptic conclusion, and we need to see restored an entire apostolic atmosphere, not the least of which is the sense of urgency and expectancy of an apocalyptic end. This cannot be for us an affectation, but a real urgency, to the point that there is an 'electricity' in our atmosphere. Our children need to be persuaded that what we are about is eminently real, and that we are not just 'attending services.'

This will only come about if they do not see a different set of parents come home from the church as they saw in the church. I am not just talking about the atmosphere in our meetings, but the atmosphere that pervades the totality of our life together as an apostolic community. Are we anticipating continually the things that shall shortly come to pass? For that very reason, we must be indifferent to the various fads and fashions of our generation. The world's fashions are going to pass away. Have we come to the place where we are not moved by things? Yes, we can handle them and use them, but they do not move us. We do not all of a sudden collapse when they are removed from us.

As I have said before, we will never come to this apostolic standard by ourselves. The church is God's provision for the strength, the prayer, and the support in breaking the powers of the world in the lives of believers who intend to come to this apostolic place where: "I do not consider my life of any account as dear to myself...." We need each other to come to that emancipation, and it only comes through the true relationship which true church is. Community or life together is the provision of God, having the

155

potential to break the powers of the world that are upon us. Do you remember how Paul said that he groaned in 'this earthly tent,' and how much he desired to be with the Lord? But for 'your sakes' he was willing to abide in this flesh. He was a heavenly man; nothing was dear unto himself, that he might finish his course with joy, and the ministry that he had received of the Lord.

In 1 Thessalonians 2:10 Paul states:

> *"You are witnesses, and so is God, how devoutly and uprightly and blamelessly we behaved toward you believers."*

There is an extreme apostolic consciousness of God as witness, an awareness that before Him we are utterly transparent. God sees us in our public moments as well as our private moments. He sees us at all times, and our lives must be consciously lived in His sight. This is the only true motivation for blamelessness, and we shall never be blameless until we have it. The way we so often conduct ourselves privately and personally is a remarkable effrontery toward God. In most cases, it is really a statement to the fact that we do not believe that our lives are being lived in His sight!

It is amazing how much indulgence we allow ourselves. I am not just talking about the blatant sin. That can be sufficient to contradict our entire testimony, and to indicate to the principalities and powers of the air that we are not to be feared. I am speaking about something even yet deeper than that. Paul speaks about having a conscience without offense toward God and toward men. Indulgence can take the form of continually thinking our own thoughts when we are free to think our own thoughts, critical thoughts, selfish thoughts, and resentful thoughts. They are just as ungodly as the act of fornication or some other gross sin. The apostle is the thing in himself. Through and through, the incarnate word of Truth, the whole truth and nothing but the truth. Even in his private and personal thoughts, he is conscious of a God in whose sight he is utterly transparent.

Paul said, *"You are witnesses, and so is God, how devotedly and uprightly and blamelessly we behaved toward you believers."*

The apostolic requirement is far beyond the mere outward conduct; it requires the integrity of the total man— spirit, soul and body. Paul was truly a man who was bound in the Spirit going toward Jerusalem. This needs to be a description of us as well. I am not saying these things to bring us under any condemnation, but rather to show us how high the standard of excellence is that God calls apostolic. It must be so, for it is the standard that is the plumb-line from heaven to earth. It is the ladder that connects heaven and earth, the standard for an unbelieving world, against which all things are to be measured. That is apostolic, and it is God's intention for the church in every place.

The incentive, therefore, for holiness and blamelessness is always set in the consciousness of God as a Judge. That is why Paul could speak with full conviction to the Athenians, *"God has appointed a day in which he will judge all nations."* I can just see the cold chill coming up the spines of those unbelieving philosophers. They had never before heard such a concept. But, it only requires one hearing when it comes from the lips of an apostolic man who is not just merely speaking a technicality of doctrine, but who awesomely knows the Judge. That is why Paul says, "Knowing the terror of God, I persuade men." *"It is a fearful thing to fall into the hands of the living God."* How is it that Paul knows it, and we do not? He knows it by relationship, and by the intimacy of His knowledge of God, and this is the deepest of all apostolic requirements.

THE YOKE OF THE LORD

"Take My yoke upon you and learn of Me for I am meek and lowly," said Jesus.

157

Are we with God, or are we freewheeling, independent agents who come and go as we please? Is our language, "Well, I think I'll attend this conference, or go to that college. I will see how I feel about coming to the meeting tonight"? If that is so, we have a greater regard for our lives than we think, and it will keep us from being apostolic.

We will never come to 'apostolic blamelessness' as long as we are self-conscious with each other. As long as we continue to live out our life in the standard that is established in our relationship with each other, rather than as a life lived unto God, then we will fall short of His intention and glory. We are going to be required to stand alone often. We are going to suffer withering blasts of reproach and criticism, and if our praise and esteem is of men, we will not stand. But if our praise is of God, and we can wait for it, then we will stand, and stand apostolically! This dependency of looking toward men for confirmation, for support, for acceptance, and for approval, needs powerfully to be broken. There is only one thing that can break it, namely, the approbation and approval that only comes from God. If we have lived habitually in the light of the response of men, needing their approval, we will collapse. There is only one who can stand under such a blast, and that is a man who lives for one satisfaction only– the praise that is not of men, but of God.

We are not going to obtain this in a day, but we will not obtain it at all if we do not consciously see it as an object to be desired above all else. We need to see the necessity of moving from our present fear of men to the restoration of the fear of God. This must be our apostolic goal and mission for which we need the participation of everyone. We are all in this together. Can you see how extraordinary and necessary the requirement of true church is? It must be the one place in the earth where we do not have to put on any appearance, where we can frankly acknowledge our defects and imperfections and speak to one another the truth in love, and exhort one another daily. Next Sunday is already too late. In fact, mere Sundays will never accomplish this. *Exhorting one another daily while it is yet today* means a radical alteration of our present lifestyle, and the establishing of a whole new set of priorities— apostolic priorities—that will make a serious intrusion upon our privacy, our pleasure, and our time.

Paul talks about being found blameless at His coming. He says that others may strive for a corruptible crown, but we for an incorruptible one. For Paul, this is absolutely vivid and real. For him, there is a shameful thing that cannot be considered, namely, that he should come before the Lord and not have a crown to lay at His feet. Do we have any desire to win a crown? The crown of glory shall not exceed the crown of our suffering! If we are unwilling for the crown of thorns, the trials, the demands, the reproaches, and the sufferings for righteousness' sake to learn what it means to live a heavenly life in an earth that is inhospitable, then we shall not have a crown to lay before Him.

The Lord Himself urges us to set our affections on the things 'above' where our treasure is. Heaven is not just biblical poetry, but the most practical and real exhortation to be blameless at His appearing. The words, *"Be ye perfect as your Father in heaven is perfect,"* ring in our ears. It is an absolute and apostolic standard much like being found blameless at His appearing, and if we will not insist upon that standard, then we quickly make 'allowances' for ourselves.

Do we have a conscience that is without offense to God and to men? What a condition to be in! It is nothing less than our re-entry into the Garden of Eden, a return to innocence. It is to be without guile, a light in the earth. It is God's invitation to us, not only in our outward conduct, but also in what we are inwardly and privately, even in the thoughts that we think, when we are free to think what we will. This requires a 'community' of the saints that is conducive to all these things. It requires a community that *speaks the truth in love* that it *might grow up unto Him in all things*. It is the end of passivity in the church, and a looking up to the platform while one man more or less conducts the whole service. We need to find and make room to speak face-to-face, not to the back of each other's heads, but seeing in each other's faces the glory of God, and moving *from glory to glory, even as by the Spirit of God.*

God's provision for the perfecting of the saints are the saints themselves in true relationship, in interaction, in confrontation, in exhortation, and in *speaking the truth in love.* We must return to these daily church realities if we are to *grow up into Him in all things, who is the Head, even Christ.* This kind of matrix of living will open our lives up, and place us under review as to just what we are about in God. It is a necessary review that has the potential to pave the way for true apostolic living.

This kind of sacramental living must be brought back into the church. We must be saved from mere expediency. It is not enough if something functions, or serves, or simply fulfils the utility and requirement of the hour. That may indeed satisfy the world's requirement, but not God's! The issue is not whether it functions. We need to see beyond utility and into the realm of glory, in things large and small. We need again to do all things as unto the Lord, *being steadfast and immovable, always abounding in the work of the Lord*, and standing fast in the faith.

CONCLUSION

This is only a little gleaning from the vineyard of Paul – just a chance phrase here and there, as it comes to us in the most superficial examination of his epistles, but what a standard begins to emerge! It is the apostolic standard that Paul himself walked in, and exhibited. *"Follow me, be imitators of me,"* needs to be said again by 'apostolic' men and women of our own age. God calls us to something even more frightening than that, namely, to be able to say with Jesus to an unbelieving world, *"If you see me, you have seen the Father. I and the Father are one."* If you want to know what God is like, then see this humility, see this uncompromising truth, see this integrity, see this righteousness, see this godly character, for this is the foundation of the church. Our power and authority in ministry are not something unrelated to it, but altogether divinely joined.

> *"For our gospel did not come to you in word only, but also in power and in the Holy Spirit and with full conviction; just as you know what kind of men we proved to be among you for your sake."*[9]

How many will subscribe to that standard from this day forth? If we are serious, we will find ourselves able to say with Paul, 'our' gospel, the gospel of His grace. It will no longer be a word of technicality, but a deeply experienced enablement for those who will *be holy as He is holy, and perfect as He is perfect.*

You also became imitators of us and of the Lord." Paul is here intimating that to follow him was to follow the Lord. That is either arrogance or the simple truth in all humility. Apostolic is the Lord in all of the incarnate fullness occupying the human frame. Can you imagine a church like that, a whole church from top to bottom, in the same apostolic splendor, the same apostolic stature, the same apostolic character, the same apostolic witness, and the same apostolic power? That is what God is wanting. Amen.

From the book, Apostolic Foundations by Art Katz Copyright (C) 2009 – Art Katz Ministries www.artkatzministries.org

---

[9] 1 Thessalonians 1:5

Made in the USA
Lexington, KY
23 May 2016